NO CROSS NO CROWN

Trust God Through the Battle

CHARLENA E. JACKSON

Mobile, Alabama

ISBN 978-1-58169-666-0
For Worldwide Distribution
Printed in the U.S.A.

Gazelle Press
P.O. Box 191540 • Mobile, AL 36619

CONTENTS

Introduction   *v*

1   Failure Is Growth   *1*

2   Foundation of Life   *10*

3   Pain Is Not the Enemy   *23*

4   Greatest Moments   *33*

5   Father Is With Me   *45*

6   Gift of Tears   *57*

7   Calming the Storm   *66*

8   Facing the Impossible   *79*

9   One Step Closer   *89*

10   Unwelcome Visitors   *100*

11   A Season for Everything   *111*

12   The Meaning of Forgiveness   *120*

13   Source of Hope   *130*

14   Embracing Change   *139*

To my beloved children
Xavier, Sarah, and Elijah:
Remember, God should always be
the solid foundation in your life.
You can never go wrong,
if you always let God lead the way
as you follow.

To my devoted grandmother, Frances E. Miles,
who is filled with so much wisdom
and who always reminded me
if I do not carry my cross,
I will not earn a crown.

INTRODUCTION

"For I know the plans I have for you," declares the LORD, *"Plans to prosper you and not to harm you, plans to give you hope and a future"* (Jeremiah 29:11).

Life is full of surprises. We find ourselves free-falling as we love freely; rejoicing in giving and not looking for anything in return; smiling without expecting to grieve; laughing not knowing pain is right around the corner. When clouds begin to block the sunlight and the storm is on the way, we move toward shelter because we know that when it rains, it pours. When rain destroys the life we have built, it is hard for some of us to start over. We may think starting over is a bad thing; however, we never take time out to have a clear understanding of why the rain took its course. We begin to think the worst of a bad situation because the thunder shook our confidence, the lightning struck our fears into action, the rain flooded our happiness, and the clouds clouded our train of thought to the point we cannot think clearly.

Sometimes we find ourselves headed down a one-way street; sooner or later we have to make a decision to turn left or right. We need to take the right steps, and use the advantage of the clouds so we can see clearly because the sun can be too bright and hinder our ability to see. That is when we have to step back, reevaluate our life, and understand the meaning of *No Cross No Crown*.

∾1∾

FAILURE IS GROWTH

Have I not commanded you? Be strong and courageous. Do not be afraid; do not be discouraged, for the LORD your God will be with you wherever you go (Joshua 1:9).

Many times in my life I have felt like I was at a dead end; plenty of times I had to turn around and go back. Sometimes I wasn't sure which crossroad to take or felt like I was headed down a one-way street. As I became wiser, I began to ask God to lead the way as I followed. When I let Him lead the way, it wasn't always peaches and cream, it was a test of my faith.

True worshipers will worship the Father in the Spirit and in truth, for they are the kind of worshipers the Father seeks (John 4:23).

Every now and then I came across a couple of flowers and took some time to smell them; however, it wasn't always a field full of lilies. I had my share of dry soil and brittle grass because I had too much sunlight that blocked my view. That was when God showered my life with rain to remove the residue. We always think that the grass is so much greener on the other side when we look at other people's lives, but in order for grass to become greener we need some showers of rain. If not, the sun will dry out the foundations in our life.

We look at failure in a negative way as an injustice and a disappointment. However, failure gives us the opportunity to look at ourselves and realize we are human. We allow failure to get the best of us, instead of looking at it as a start to a new beginning. Failure can be a blessing because it allows us to get right back up and try again.

But now, Lord, what do I look for? My hope is in you (Psalm 39:7).

My failures caused me to start over from ground zero. I was distracted, had lost hope, and wanted to give up. I even questioned God and asked Him, "Why me? What have I done to deserve such treatment? Why am I being ignored and punished for trying and giving my all?" I did not understand.

No, in all these things we are more than conquerors through Him who loved us (Romans 8:37).

When I was a freshman in college, I advised a friend to apply to the school I was attending. She took my advice, applied, and was accepted. I was happy for her; however, I noticed she was moving along in her classes rather swiftly and eventually graduated a year before I did. I also had another friend who began classes almost two years after I did, and she graduated before I did too. I felt like everyone was getting ahead, prospering, having a wonderful life full of joy, and everything was going their way.

I felt so unsuccessful because I was failing classes over and over again even though I went to the library in my spare time, stayed up all night studying, and studied note cards here and there whenever I had extra time on my hands. That didn't seem to be enough. I tried so hard to pass my classes and take care of my children plus handle additional responsibilities. I thought maybe I wasn't trying hard enough, or maybe college wasn't for me.

Some of my family members did not make it any easier. During family get-togethers during the holidays, they would ask, "When do you graduate?" I didn't have an answer. Some would make disparaging comments such as, "You've been an undergraduate for over a decade. You have too many children, how in the world are you going to finish college?"

They really thought I was living in a fantasy world. What they failed to realize is that we all should have a sense of imagination. My failures made me dream harder because I had a vision. "Where there is no vision, the people perish" (Proverbs 29:18). I visualized what I wanted and I was determined to have it. God and my imagination were my blueprints, and I proceeded to follow them with action.

After I failed my classes numerous times, I had to rejuvenate so I fasted and prayed.

Let the words of my mouth and the meditation of my heart be acceptable in Your sight, O Lord, my rock and my Redeemer (Psalm 19:14).

I changed my strategy, set new goals, and faced my challenges with a positive mindset of courage and optimism.

It might have taken longer than expected, but God had a plan for me in His time. When I felt like throwing in the towel, their senseless comments gave me a burst of energy and encouraged me to keep going.

It took me just about a decade to graduate. I might have failed some classes multiple times, but when I look back at the sacrifices I had to make, it was well worth it. My children did not have to raise themselves. I was there to see my children's milestones—their first words and steps. I wiped their tears from a fall or when they were crying for no reason. I was there to see them smile and laugh, to hear them giggle, to tuck them in at night, help them get ready in the morning, and feed and clothe them. I cradled them in my arms and most importantly spent time loving them unconditionally. Those were the sacrifices I made, and I would not have it any other way.

My failures taught me to completely trust in God because dropping out of school was not an option. It made me realize God is bigger than the situation, and man's words should not make me second guess my destiny.

Therefore I tell you, whatever you ask for in prayer, believe that you have received it, and it will be yours (Mark 11:24).

As I faced the challenges resulting from my failures, my frame of thinking improved. It changed my mood into a positive outlook, and the knowledge I gained made me appreciate my failures because they made me who I am today. My failures created an appetite to fulfill my destiny.

Failure taught me not to accept no as a final answer; instead, it helped me to improve my strategy, dissect the definition of growth, and eliminate any thoughts of giving up regardless of how many times I had to go back to the drawing board. It spurred me on to create a positive mindset and not to settle for less. It gave me the push I needed to make room for improvement to execute my plan.

Guide me in Your truth and teach me, for You are God my Savior, and my hope is in You all day long (Psalm 25:5).

In spite of occasional failures, we all can make room for growth in a positive way. When we think we have failed, we become depressed and sidetracked; we want to give up.

Failure is a valuable teacher that we should always appreciate because it teaches us how to be patient and to wait for the approval from our heavenly Father.

This is my second time writing *No Cross No Crown: Trust God Through the Battle.* The first time I wrote it, I thought it was an awesome book. I worked on it morning and evening. I had note cards, pens, pencils, and paper beside my bed, just in case I thought of something to write about while I was sleeping. I used to wake up, write things down, and head right back to sleep. I was so dedicated as I worked on it day in and day out.

Then one day, I upgraded my computer and lost my file. What was so strange about the situation was that I had saved the book to my hard drive and two USB drives, and had sent it to all three of my email accounts. However, I could not open the document in any of my files or emails.

All my other documents, pictures, and videos were saved and transferred over to the new upgraded software that was installed on my computer and the USB drives I saved them on, but the document and file from my book was gone. I sent the documents to my sister and a good friend of mine to ask if they could open the file, but only three pages were saved out of two hundred.

I was hurt, disappointed, and thought I failed myself and God because I had put so much work into my book. Half of the introduction was saved, and half of the chapter "Pain Is Not the Enemy" was saved.

After I had a pity party for a couple days, I asked God to use me according to His will. From that day on, I made up my mind to let Him guide my thoughts and my fingers on the keyboard, and to let Him lead the way as I devoted myself to writing it once again.

I look at failure as preparing me for my journey and improving my life for the better. When I was a junior in college, four times I failed a class called "Vertebrate Physiology." I knew the material; however, the exams were complicated. My professor was difficult, and sometimes I felt he was being difficult on purpose. Although I failed his class four times, I was not going to give up. Failure was not an option. I had to pass Vertebrate Physiology to graduate.

During the summer, I worked hard; I recorded every lecture and lab. Instead of studying directly from his notes, I studied what he did not cover. Before class I made a list of words out of the word "failure." I turned a negative word into a positive outlook. It broadened my mind during the quarter to seek hope and to earn a passing grade at the end.

Let's dissect and break down the word "failure." Failure will give us an earful of noise, but it is up to us to listen and observe. Failure can flare up any circumstance more than what it appears to be; having faith can calm it down easily. Faith can turn our life around and eliminate our fear. Failure will challenge our faith, and it will show us God is real. Failure will give us the fuel we need to keep going because it is not accepted in God's plan.

After all, failure is growth and it can develop patience in us. It changes our lives to want to do better. Everyone has room for personal growth when they're thinking and moving in a positive direction.

> *Consider it pure joy, my brothers and sisters, whenever you face trials of many kinds, because you know that the testing of your faith produces perseverance. Let perseverance finish its works so that you may be mature and complete not lacking anything* (James 1:2-4).

What begins as failure can be transformed into blessings and a new outlook at life. A right look at our trials will open our eyes to see that God is real. He will open our ears to hear the devil is a liar and that he has no choice but to flee from us. God will give us the fuel we need to light our fire. He is a fair and honest God; we should fear no one but Him.

Sometimes we feel like we have it all together. Then there are days when we feel like a leaf that has fallen from a tree and is blowing in the wind, not knowing where it will land. However, God knows, and we are so precious to Him. He catches us and gently puts us in a safe place.

Failure should not make us bitter, nor should it make us want to give up. It should make us brighter and wiser. We need to know that God loves us so much that He only wants the best for us.

Failure does not mean defeat. It is not God's will; however, we will face trials and tribulations in life. Challenges and setbacks can weigh us down. We should not give up but keep moving, pushing, and knowing that all things work together for the good. We need to be willing to do better and gain insight from what went wrong.

We should not let failure produce fear and its emotional and physical effects. Fear is destruction, the negative emotion of darkness and the great destroyer. God does not intend for us to live in fear, whether it is to fear man or a situation. Fear is destructive and it will cause a person to become sick from being stressed, worried, or jealous out of hatred, greediness, and selfishness. Sickness is not in God's plan.

And the prayer offered in faith will make the sick person well; the Lord will raise them up. If they have sinned, they will be forgiven (James 5:15).

God wants us to have a relationship and communicate with Him. He wants us to be filled with love, expectation, hope, and anticipation.

Lord, all my desires is before You; And my sighing is not hidden from you (Psalm 38:9).

What we need to understand is that He is waiting for us to come to Him. When we communicate with Him, our words set up patterns of action, and as a result, God is going to do what He think is best for us.

When we do not understand our failures, the most important word we should always remember is the acronym of A.S.K.

Ask and it will be given to you; Seek and you will find; Knock and the door will be opened to you. For everyone who asks receives; the one who seeks finds; and the one who knocks, the door will be opened (Matthew 7:7-8).

God is a miracle worker and He wants the best for us; however, we have to remember to A.S.K. God for His guidance and for direction. He knows our every thought, pain, and desire. If we ask, He will be there to give an answer because He is an on-time loving God.

The most important principles I've learned from failure are to have good communication and a relationship with God, and to concentrate and focus on His plan for me. They helped me to open my eyes and see the bigger picture. They made me realize anything that is worth having may require me to fail numerous times in order to know exactly what I want. Most of the time, if it is easy for someone to give up or quit, it is probably not what they want to do.

Failure gave me a headway on solving my problems and

achieving my goals. It helped me to educate my children to prepare them for possible setbacks and how to overcome what they might think is failure.

We should always control our thoughts and turn negative thinking into a positive one in order to make corrections that will help us build confidence to keep going. Failure prepares us to meet life challenges as we face each obstacle and overcome them by earning the crown from the cross we bear.

Make failure a concentration of the will—the will to want to continue moving forward and the will to have the ability to execute anything you set your mind to do. Failure stops procrastination because it will make us execute the journey God has planned for us to achieve our goals. Last but not least, failure opens our eyes to see we are never alone and it produces great leaders. Keep praying because God is listening, and He is with us every step of our journey.

Dear Heavenly Father, the Beginning and the End, the First and the Last, our amazing God who has all the power to diminish our fear and calm our soul,

We humbly ask You to help us to face our fears and to stand firm in the mist of the battles that we may consider failures. For You, Lord, know all things work together for good. Thank You for Your unconditional love that is filled with peace and for Your grace and mercy. Amen.

❧ 2 ❧

FOUNDATION OF LIFE

For no one can lay any foundation other than the one already laid, which is Christ (1 Corinthians 3:11).

Throughout my life people have always called me a "tough cookie." However, I do not consider myself a tough cookie because a cookie tends to break; and when it breaks, it turns into crumbs that you cannot put back together. God is my structured foundation. I may crack, but because He is my source, my strength, and my all, I do not break apart. When mistakes try to take me down, God builds me up by creating another layer of tough, thicker skin.

We all have made mistakes that were not pleasing to God and fallen short from receiving His grace and mercy. Let us not forget that God is a forgiving God, and His mercy endures forever. God does not want our mistakes to destroy our character, nor does He want us to be filled with regrets. However, we should not make an excuse for our mistakes; instead, we should learn from the resulting lessons and consequences we had to pay.

When I used to ask myself, if I had an opportunity to go back in time what would I change, I always came up with so many things. Nowadays, when I ask myself that question, my answer is that I would not change anything at all. My mistakes helped me to become closer to God and to see I cannot pave the foundation of my life. After making the same mistakes over and over again, surely it could be said I learned the hard way. As I repented from my mistakes, the cracks started to seal, and that is when I realized God is my foundation.

As we make mistakes, we have the opportunity to either learn from them as they teach us a lesson or wallow in our mess. Mistakes can help us grow, become wiser, and create a stronger bond with God. Furthermore, they teach us to learn so much about ourselves. Mistakes help us to set boundaries, and to know when to pick and choose our battles.

Mistake is another word for transformation. Did the mistakes that you have made in your life transform you to be a better person? Did the transformation promote growth, persistence, and the ability to press forward? Does the word "mistake" seem more like a friend who has your best interests at heart or a foe that wants you to fail? If we count our blessings and do not look at our mistakes as failures, they should change our life for the better. It all depends on us. If we answered no to the above questions, we need to sit back and look over our life. We should not let our mistakes define us as a person in a negative way. We have the ability to turn our negative thinking into positive.

In order to lay a strong foundation, we must maintain our faith in God. If not, our foundation will not only crack, but it will cave in because our foundation is not built on the Rock. God, in fact, lays the foundation for us, and He gives us the supplies we need to build upon it solidly; we just need to know how to use them correctly. You might be asking, how do I start the process of building on my foundation? In order to use the supplies the correct way, you must read and have an understanding of God's Word. Your soul will be renewed, your spirit and flesh will be cleansed, and your journey and walk with God will be the beginning of everlasting life!

As we let the Father order our footsteps, He will lay out our foundation. The growth and building will start from there. Trust in Him because He will never break His promises.

Giving our life and soul to Christ doesn't mean we will not have pain, trials, tribulations, or suffering; indeed, we will have all of the above. He loves us so much to the point where our pain does not compare to the backstabbing, trials, struggles, tribulations, false conviction, brutal execution, and challenges Christ had to bear and face on the cross.

The soldiers twisted together a crown of thorns and put it on His head. They clothed Him in a purple robe. And went up to Him again and again, saying, "Hail, King of the Jews!" And they slapped Him in the face (John 19:2-3).

Christ was betrayed and denied because He was the Son of God. His enemies tried to destroy Him; however, Christ kept pushing through because He loves us so much! They tried to place fear in His heart and that did not work. He asked, "God why have You forsaken me?" However, He also said, "God forgive them for they do not know what they do." We serve a mighty God!

They brutally beat Him until His back was bloody with many stripes; however, their mission was not accomplished. "Instead, one of the soldiers pierced Christ side with a spear, bringing a sudden flow of blood and water" (John 19:34). Christ fell a couple times, but He got right back up because He loves us! Christ had to carry His cross after He was beaten. Then they nailed Him to the cross, on which He suffered and died for us.

No foundation could be any firmer, stronger, have more stability, or be more balanced than Christ! He is the deepest core of our foundation.

> *On the first day of the week, very early in the morning, the women took the spices they had prepared and went to the tomb. They found the stone rolled away from the tomb, but when they entered, they did not find the body of the Lord Jesus. While they were wondering about this, suddenly two men in clothes that gleamed like lighting stood beside them. In their fright the women bowed down their faces to the ground, but the men said to them. "Why do you look for the living among the dead? He is not here; He has risen! Remember how He told you, while He was still with you in Galilee: 'The Son of Man must be delivered over to the hands of sinners, be crucified and on the third day be raised again.'" Then they remembered His words* (Luke 24: 1:8).

We serve an amazing God! Yes, we are going to have hardships and pain, but we have to remember we serve a God who has all power in His hands, and there is not a thing too hard for Him. He is an on-time God. When we are being tested, God is preparing to use us, and He is renewing our strength.

We have to learn how to ask God to use us according to His will and know regardless of what we go through, God will not let any harm come to us because He is our Protector, our Shield, and Comforter in both good and bad times. He uses it all together for our good and His glory.

Let's look at the story of Job. He was a God-fearing man, and he had everything he could ever ask for: a lovely family, a wife, seven sons, and three daughters. Job owned thousands of sheep and camels, hundreds of oxen and donkeys, and he had many servants. He was an awesome man among his neighbors, willing to love and share his blessings from God. He spoke highly of God at all times. God had confidence in Job, and He knew He was the solid foundation in Job's life. God gave Satan permission to test Job's faith; however, He told Satan that he could not touch Job. Satan was more than sure his mission was going to be easy.

> *"Does Job fear God for nothing?" Satan replied. "Have you not put a hedge around him and his household and everything else he has? You have blessed the work of his hands, so that his flocks and herds are spread throughout the land. But now stretch out your hand and strike everything he has, and he will surely curse you to your face." The Lord said to Satan, "Very well, then, everything he has is in your power, but on the man himself do not lay a finger"* (Job 1:9-12).

God took everything from Job: his oxen and donkeys wandered off, his sheep and servants were burned, his camels were stolen, some of his servants were killed, and all of his children died.

But after all was said and done, Job did not curse God; he prepared himself for his death and praised the Lord. Satan did not think God took enough away or tortured Job enough.

> *"Skin for skin!" Satan replied. "A man will give all he has for his own life. But now stretch out your hand and strike his flesh and bones, and he will surely cruse you to your face." The Lord said to Satan, "Very well, then, he is in your hands; but you must spare his life"* (Job 2:4-6).

Satan intentionally afflicted Job with sores that were painful from the crown of his head to the soles of his feet. Job's wife told him to curse God and die. His friends sat with him for seven days and did not say a word, although eventually they questioned his motives and walked away. During the midst of being tested, Job kept praying, but he grew weary.

> How long will you torment me and crush me with words? Ten times now you have reproached me; shamelessly you attacked me. Though I cry, "Violence!" I get no response; though I call for help, there is no justice. He has alienated my family from me; my relatives have gone away; and my closest friends have forgotten me (Job 19: 2-3; 7, 13-15).

Job did not have any idea why this was happening to him. However, God sustained Job's faith and kept him faithful. He knew Job was going to pass the test. During his years of suffering, Job kept the faith because God was his solid foundation.

When we go through trials and tribulations, it doesn't mean we have to give up, drown, and sink to the bottom. The trials we face in life are helping us build upon His foundation. Ask God to be your life jacket to keep you afloat. Many times in my life, I felt like I was dealt a sour, bitter, cruel, and unjust hand. In the midst of troubled waters, my head was barely above water, but God was my life jacket.

Having God as my life jacket taught me the definition of survival. Instead of doubting, thinking the worst, and complaining, I had to shift gears to survival mode. Survival mode released perseverance, persistency, and endurance. Negative thoughts produced negative energy; negative thinking made me wallow in self-pity, drained my confidence, and made me brittle and fatigued. It made my situations worse than what they really were. I had a choice to either let negative thoughts and negative energy transform my life or to make the best out of my situation.

When I decided to let God be my life jacket, I felt a huge

relief of burden lifted off of me. Not only did He keep me afloat, but He gave me strength to swim. As I gained strength, over time God's grace and mercy gave me a clear understanding that every situation I was going through would turn out for the better.

It is by grace you have been saved (Ephesians 2:4-5).

One morning my children and I were getting ready for work and school. I was starting a new job, and I was very excited. I received a call from an officer asking me if I drove a Chevrolet Cavalier. As I replied yes, I looked out the window and saw my car was not there. I yelled, "My car is gone!" The officer said, "Yes ma'am, that is why I am calling you. We found your car slammed into a tree. However, we also have the driver because he was transported to the hospital."

I was in shock that my car was stolen. I started to panic, thinking, "How I am going to get around, and how are my children going to get to school?" I then thought, *Goodness, today is the first day of work, and first impressions are important.*

I was thinking of everything I could think of, but not thinking of God's ability to handle it. The officer told me to call 911 to file a police report. Before I did, I lit seven white candles for harmony and one blue candle for peace. I was calmed and relaxed. I prayed and asked God to join me in prayer because I wanted to feel His presence.

I prayed for guidance, peace, understanding, and I also prayed for the thief who stole my car. I prayed for him because God had prepared me for this situation during the night. I had tossed and turned and could not sleep because I was so restless. I was not going to give the devil credit for my discomfort, so I turned negative thoughts into positive ones.

I got up and stretched so my body could relax, struck a match to light a candle, and started my devotion. I read my Bible and asked God to guide my footsteps throughout the coming day. I always read a devotional to bring peace to my mind, soul, and spirit. The title for my devotion was *Believing in Advance* and the Scripture was, "Surely I am coming quickly" (Revelation 22:20) followed by an urgent, echoing prayer, "Amen. Even so, come, Lord Jesus!" God has a way of speaking to you and through you by your actions.

I had not been able to sleep that night because He knew someone was going to steal my car, and He had to prepare me to trust in Him when the situation was revealed to me. He spoke to me through His words, and His words gave me comfort because my heart and mind were at peace.

After I meditated and read the Word, I called 911 to file the police report. The officer checked out the scene and he asked me if I knew the person who stole my car. I looked at him with a blank stare because I was saying to myself, "You're kidding me, right?" I paused for a couple seconds and said, "No. I do not know who stole my car." He said, "I asked because you are so calm, and I figured you knew the person."

I then said, "I am calm because God already prepared me for this situation this morning. Instead of running around yelling, filled with rage, fear, and a possibility of having a stroke or a heart attack, I chose to believe in advance to let God handle this issue because it is out of my control."

The officer looked at me as if I were crazy and said, "Hmmm. Okay. So you do not know this person, correct?" I said, "Correct." The officer gave me the police report number and said, "Good luck with everything." I kindly said, "Thank you, many blessings are going to come out of this situation."

The officer again looked at me as if I were crazy. I smiled and told him to have a blessed day.

I knew this was going to be a challenging situation; however, I also knew if I handled it according to God's will, He would be with me every step of the way. In order to build on our foundation to make it strong, we must face our trials head on without hesitation.

There are going to be difficult hills to climb, and we might slip, but we have to know that God has a good grip on us and He will pull us up at the right time. In the midst of it all, He is saying, "My child, I've got you." We must believe as Job believed in God. God sits up on high and He looks down low; He sees it all, and He knows how much we can bear.

Keep the faith, keep praying, keep believing, and know God is our solid foundation and our bridge over troubled waters.

I know what it is to be in need, and I know what it is to have plenty. I have learned the secret of being content in any and every situation, whether well fed or hungry, whether living in plenty or in want. I can do all this through him who gives me strength (Philippians 4:12-13).

Later that morning, I asked for help from a select few family members. From the tone in their voices it seemed as if they were happy to hear my car was stolen. When I asked them if they could take me to get a rental car, their tone changed, and they started to huff and puff. I said in a calm tone, "Thank you, but never mind."

It's funny how news travels fast. Soon everyone was calling me, but not one person offered to lend a helping hand. I called my supervisor and told her what happened, and she understood. I called my insurance company to get information on how to get a rental, and they gave me the information I needed.

God is so good, and it shows He is an on-time God. I called Enterprise and they made the process easy; they gathered my information and offered to come pick me up. God always makes a way out of no way.

> *Do not be anxious about anything, but in every situation, by prayer and petition, with thanksgiving, present your request to God* (Philippians 4:6).

The rest of the week I was so busy working, trying to find a car, and taking care of my responsibilities that I thought I was going to go insane. I began to feel resentment towards the person who stole my car. I went to the impound company, but I could not get anything out of my car because I was told I had to get a release of property form from the courthouse.

When I went to the courthouse to get the form, I was told my ID was not good enough—I needed a copy of my car title, which was in the car. I had to drive back home, which was about an hour away, to get the original title and then go back to the courthouse to get the form approved. After it was approved, the impound company was closed. I was surprised to see an impound company closed at 5 p.m. Normally an impound company stays open 24 hours.

The next day, I had to get the youngest children together for school, go to work, and squeeze in time to go back to the impound company to take care of business.

While my oldest son and I were grieving over Red Rose (our pet name for the car), we cleaned the car out and took what was left. It was too much to endure. The front end of the car was smashed in, the two front wheels were barely hanging on, the windshield was shattered, the air bags were released, and the driver and passenger side doors could not close. Needless to say, Red Rose was completely totaled. God's grace and mercy were with the thief. Someone else was with him because you could see the crown of someone's head had molded into the windshield. That person must have hit the windshield pretty hard.

I looked at more than twenty used cars and none of them were suitable or safe. My mechanic gave me insight on what kind of car I should look for. He was on the phone telling me what to say, and finally I found the right car. However, it was too expensive—nine thousand dollars.

I hesitated because it was over my budget. I had to take care of my children and I had bills to pay. My insurance said that Red Rose was worth only two thousand dollars. That left me with seven thousand dollars that I had to come up with out of pocket. I had a refund check in route, but I already had made plans for that money.

I heard God say, "Trust Me," but I thought I was hearing things. Nevertheless, He always has a way of revealing Himself either through people, music, words, or any other way possible to get my attention. The car broker's phone started ringing, and my friend and I looked up at the sky. The broker's phone sounded like heaven's gates were opening. He said, "My ring tone is called *Heaven Is Calling*."

I knew right then and there that God was speaking to me. I walked by faith, not by sight, and realized I had to sacrifice.

Trust in the LORD with all of your heart and lean not on your own understanding; in all your ways submit to Him, and He will make your paths straight (Proverbs 3:5-6).

I wasn't going to be able to use the refund money for the

plans I made, which was to catch up on my credit card bills.

I had to go back and forth to the courthouse to submit paper work. Weeks later, documents came in the mail stating a public defender was fighting for the thief to get out of jail. As I read more details, I saw he had stolen someone else's car too. I was very upset because I had to charge all my credit cards to pay my bills, pay for my books, and take care of my children. It was disappointing I had to go through all of that, just for him to get out of jail without any consequences. He only served two months for stealing my car because the judge pronounced his sentence as time served. Now it is three years later, and I still have not received a penny of restitution.

If God wasn't the foundation and the source of my life, I would not have known which way to turn when I was going through trials, tribulations, and making sacrifices to survive. I was not only thinking about myself, I had to make wise decisions for my children. I had sleepless nights and struggled with my bills. They were not always paid on time, but they were paid before the month was out. Most of my days were rough, but God gave me the strength I needed to make it through another day.

During our trials, God gives us strength to carry our cross. When we have to suit up to carry another cross, God is right there to help us. He will be there working in our favor at all times; although it is rough, God knows exactly what He is doing.

He will be there to pull us up when we are slipping and falling. He listens to us and gives us the answers to the questions that burden us. He cradles us in His arms when we are worried and weary. Through it all, our foundation might crack, but it will remain stable because we maintain our faith in God. He will be there paving another layer, bit by bit, piece by piece sealing up the cracks to make it stronger and secured.

Dearly Heavenly Father,

Thank You, for being the foundation of our lives. We ask, Lord, when the going gets tough, please give us the strength to call on Your deserving name. Help us to realize our mistakes can be fixed and that everything happens for a reason and not by chance. We humbly ask, dear heavenly Father, not to move the mountains out of our way but to give us the strength, endurance, and courage to climb each mountain. Most generous Father, we ask You to cover us from the crown of our heads to the soles of our feet. Amen.

In chapter four you will see how God worked this car situation for the good and blessed us.

❧3❧

PAIN IS NOT THE ENEMY

I will praise Your name, O Lord, for it is good, For You have rescued me from my troubles and helped me to triumph over my enemies (Psalm 54:6-7).

When we think of pain, what comes to mind? Hurt from a broken heart? Suffering because we continue to try and give it our all, yet things never fall into place? Agony from being in an unhealthy relationship and/or friendship, working at a job that doesn't appreciate us, our children refusing to listen when we only want the best for them? Maybe it's torture from being jabbed here, there, everywhere from friends, family, and life situations, and the sense that nothing is going to get any better.

Some would say that pain is an ache and discomfort that seem to never go away no matter how hard we try to keep a positive attitude or keep moving forward. Pain is frowned upon because we think it is the master of negative energy that causes tears, sorrow, grief, and confusion. It does cause one to make a confession out of being hurt, having feelings of guilt and pity, and being deeply wounded.

Pain can be damaging to our mind mentally; it will cause us to withdraw from others due to our discomfort and suffering. Feeling unpleasant, rejected, fearing change, having financial worries and embarrassment are all signs of pain.

Pain can make us feel numb, vulnerable, and helpless. Our reaction to it can change our character from sweet to bitter; shift our attitude from fruitful to sour; or make us want to give up, to think the worse of things, curse God, stop having faith, and have a negative attitude about our life and other people.

Most people think pain is the enemy. I must say that I see why one would think like that. I've been down that road so many times, but I had to finally ask myself, is pain my enemy? Now I look at failure and pain as my best friends because they have been there with me through my ups and downs, thick and thin. Each tear I cried due to my suffering, struggles, hurt, and pain helped me create thicker skin and learn more about myself.

When my son was being bullied in kindergarten through the third grade, mostly by the same person, I was livid and felt a sense of pain in my heart. I didn't feel at ease knowing my son was stressed and unhappy due to someone inflicting pain on him, whether it was emotional or physical.

I reached out to his teachers and the administrators for years, and although they took time to listen, I felt they were not doing enough. They did not understand the pain my son endured; most importantly, I saw him as only my baby. A child should not know anything about depression or stress; he should live a joyful, happy, fun, and fulfilled childhood.

Instead my son used to come home and tell me about his day. Most of the time it was about a little boy torturing him with his words and hands. My son did not want to eat, play, or talk when he came home. He would ball up in his bed and lay there. I always comforted and talked to him, although I believed it went into one ear and out the other. I had a hard time getting him out of bed to go to school every morning.

I was very upset; as a mother I was in pain, knowing another child was sucking the life out of my son. My son loves to smile, he is friendly, playful, and very loving. On the weekends he was himself, but during the week he would turn into someone I couldn't recognize.

After two years of meeting with his teachers and the administration, I decided what they were doing wasn't enough. I also realized that there was only so much the administration could do.

I reached out to the bully's mother, making her aware of the situation. She acted as though she did not have a clue about her son bullying my son. I kindly asked her again and said, "You do not recall the administrators telling you about how your son called my son names and put hands on him?" There were many more issues I pointed out to her, but she denied every incident and said, "Well my son said your son was bullying him."

I asked if she were serious because her son was so much bigger than my son. I told her, "If that's the case, which I doubt, apparently my child is now defending himself over the course of the years of being bullied by your son." I politely told her that if her son continued to bully my son, I gave him permission to protect himself. I kindly let her know when my son took action I was not paying for any doctor bills because I have police reports about the bullying that occurred.

Next, I again reached out to the administrators filled with disappointment, thinking they were not honest with me over the past years when they had assured me the parents knew about every situation.

After I spoke with the bully's mother again, she admitted

only slightly to knowing what was going on. I didn't believe her, and right then and there, I lost respect for her. To an adult, bullying shouldn't be taken lightly, especially if you know your child is the bully. A parent has the power to nip that in the bud. However, this parent was filled with denial and did not want to know the whole truth.

I will admit that I have been in situations when the truth hurts, but I always faced up to the fact that knowing the truth was like having a weight lifted off my shoulders. Some people hate to hear the truth. I believe they look at it as a sign of failure or weakness. It is neither. It is building strength, being courageous, and accepting the fact that nobody is perfect.

The truth is the main key to solving your answers to the problems you may face.

Truth stands the test of time; lies are soon exposed (Proverbs 12: 19).

I believe part of the definition of truth should be preventing a disaster from occurring. Telling the truth and accepting the truth could save someone's life. It could save a marriage or a friendship. Telling the truth comes from courage, and it prevents destruction.

The administrators told me they were happy to know I reached out to the parent. I reassured them, after the same situation continued to occur, that there is but so much an administrator could do. In my opinion, I felt they should have expelled the child from school, but then I thought he would have bullied someone else and the cycle would have continued.

Apparently, the bully's mother eventually spoke with him because the bully stopped pushing my son around, although he started to bully another child.

The hurt and pain I felt gave me strength to write two books. One is a bullying book for children/young adults to read called *I'm Speaking Up but You Are Not Listening*. The other book is for parents/guardians/teachers/administrators, etc. and is called *Teachers Just Don't Understand*. They focus on looking out for signs and how to proceed with solving the issues of bullying.

Another result of pain in my life is that it made me realize that I have to love myself before I could love anyone else. I always found myself giving more to others, not knowing I was neglecting myself. With that being said, the ones who I always helped were the ones who inflicted pain on me. However, they failed to realize the pain I endured helped me to look deep within myself, and it taught me to open my eyes to receive pain in a positive way.

Pain helped me turn negative situations into positive ones. Now, when I help people I do it from the kindness of my heart, or I say no without regrets. I know God sees my good deed and I know I will be blessed. Pain also helped me to know when I was being misused, not being appreciated, and taken advantage of.

Most importantly, it helped me love and appreciate myself. Instead of running myself crazy and doing so much for other people, I now take time out for me. I go to the movies, take relaxing strolls in the park, read, take myself out to eat, and get a massage.

Taking care of myself made me feel at ease, comforted, and gave me a piece of mind. It was refreshing and it renewed my mind, soul, and spirit with so much positive energy.

We are afflicted in every way, but not crushed, perplexed, but not despairing, persecuted, but not forsaken; struck down but not destroyed (2 Corinthians 4:8-9).

Three years ago when I had knee surgery, I asked my siblings if one of them could take me to the hospital. One of them told me she had to go to work and wash a client's hair. She said she could drop me off and come back to pick me up. I asked how much she charged her clients and how many clients she was going to see that particular day.

I asked because I was going to pay her the same amount to take me and stay with me until my surgery was over. I had to think long and hard about the offer I was going to suggest to my sister, until I realized that I had done so much for her, not only her, but her children as well.

My oldest sister told me she had to get it approved by her job (which I understood); however, if I were her boyfriend or boyfriend's daughter, I would have gotten a definite yes when I asked. I was hurt because I have done so much for her as well as her children, without hesitation.

I sat there in tears and filled with anger. I asked God, "Why am I being neglected by my family? I am willing to help everyone, but when I need help nobody ever comes through for me." I always have a price to pay. I either had to give someone gas money or spend more money.

I was disappointed because I never asked them for gas money or money when they needed my assistance. When I looked back at how many times I helped them, I never asked for the favor to be returned.

I went out of my way to help them because it showed that I loved them, and my actions spoke louder than my words. I did not feel loved. After all I had done from my heart for them and their family, I was sure they would be there when I needed them the most.

I was so angry from feeling deceived. I blocked their numbers from calling me and chose not to have a relationship with them for a year. I must say, I was at peace for that year because I did not have anyone asking me for this or that, but my heart was not settled because I was not forgiving my siblings.

Pain is a funny thing, because pain will show us we're wrong as well.

Everyone ought to examine themselves before they eat of the bread and drink from the cup (1 Corinthians 11:28).

Does pain sound like the enemy? Pain will have you look deeper at the core; it will have you dissect yourself as a person.

When I had issues with my finances, trying to care for my children alone, I attended school to make a better living for my family. I blamed pain for shooting down my confidence. I was rejected from interviews. I was told I was either over- or under-qualified for the position. I had two interviewers tell me I would receive a promotion quickly because I was confident in my interview, and they did not want me to take their position. I was highly disappointed because my agenda wasn't to take someone's spot they had earned. I wanted to get my foot in the door to support my family.

My financial worries overpowered my concentration. Bills were coming in constantly; simple things such as paying for a field trip was a financial struggle. I knew I couldn't survive just by making ends meet from a work/study position and student loans. I applied for jobs daily. If I were invited for an interview, they either couldn't pay me my worth, I had too much education, or my personality was too bold.

I tried cutting back on things my children and I did not need; however, we really needed everything I tried to cut back on. I was running out of solutions. I made up my mind that I could not worry about what was out of my control. I continued to budget my finances and work with what I had. When I stopped worrying about what I did not have, things started to fall into place.

The director of the Physical Education Department at a college in Georgia called. She asked if I were still interested in a professor's position. Honestly, I did not remember applying for a professor's position. She said, "Ma'am, you applied for the position more than a year ago." Of course I accepted the offer.

God can use pain for good as it teaches us how to be honest with ourselves. It helps us to grow, build self-confidence, and develop a thicker skin to protect us from our enemies. Have you ever noticed how most of the time when your enemy tried to reflect pain on you, it back fired on them?

God saw it coming, cradled you in His arms, and shielded you from the pain that was intended to hurt you. Isn't God good! Many times in my life I've been deceived by pain. I felt like the pain was too strong for me to heal from it. Instead, the pain I endured was making me a stronger person in my mind, soul, and spirit. With that being said, I had to open my heart and mind to dig deeper in faith.

After I asked my siblings to take me to get knee surgery, their actions and answers were no. I felt like I did not have anyone to call; however, God always opens a door for us when we least expect it. I called my cousin, and she and her daughter were with me every step of the way without any questions asked.

Until this day I appreciate them because I never was there for them the way I was there for my siblings, but they were available when I needed them. It shows if we have faith, God will be there to catch us when we think all else has failed.

> Draw near with confidence to the throne of grace, so that we may receive mercy and find grace to help in time if need (Hebrews 4:16).

We have to be willing to receive and expect God's renewed strength.

The pains that were inflicted on me the most were through people whom I loved the most. I found a way to get through it by praying. We have to learn to put our pride aside, ask for help, and be strong enough to expect the blessings God has prepared for us.

At times it may seem as if the storm will never end. We have to keep in mind God knows and sees what we are going through. He is with us every step of the way. We have to keep the faith and take every step with joy. We should count our pain as joy because after we have endured the hurt, the pain teaches us how to love, forgive, and most importantly trust in God every step of the way.

> Take my yoke upon you and learn from me, for I am gentle and humble in heart, and you will find rest for your souls (Matthew 11:29).

Regardless of how much pain we have experienced, it cannot compare to the pain Christ sacrificed for us. He was deceived, spat on, beaten, and denied. After all the pain, hurt, and pretense, He still walked through the valley of death for our sins. He was brutally whipped and suffered as He took up the cross and carried it for our sins.

Our pain cannot compare to the different emotions Christ experienced as they nailed Him to the cross. The pain He went through leads us to be victorious! He knows our every need and the desires of our heart. Rest and be assured He is with us through it all. "Come to me, all who are weary and burdened, and I will give you rest" (Matthew 11:28).

We might think we are going through it alone, but the One who died on the cross for us is alive and well today. We may think that He has forsaken us, but He is by our side every step of the way.

Is pain the enemy? Pain heals our wounds and produces the healing word we call hope. Hope molded our tears from the pain and produced patience. Patience is the offspring that develops into trust. Trust releases the seeds to grow and live by faith and not by sight. Faith helps us to gain knowledge of God's Word. And God's Word opens our minds to feel His inner peace, grace, mercy, and unconditional love.

Pain is not meant for us to be the victim or to hurt us; it helps us grow and to look deep within ourselves. Most importantly, pain gives us the opportunity to give God all our attention, to seek His guidance and ask for His will to be done.

Dear Heavenly Father, the Healer of broken hearts,

We ask that You help us to received pain as a renewal of hope, patience, trust, and faith. Our Fighter and Protector in each battle and challenge, thank You for giving us the strength to stand tall as Your warriors. We know our armor and each step we take is secured, shielded, and covered in Your blood. Amen.

⁓4⁓

GREATEST MOMENTS

You make known to me the path of life. 'You fill me with joy in your presence, with eternal pleasures at your right hand (Psalm 16:11).

Sometimes the worst things turn out to be the greatest things that could happen. I always used to ask, "God, why me?" I felt like nothing was working out in my favor, and every time I turned around I had to suit up for another battle. We never know what God has in store and sometimes we question Him. However, during our greatest trials He is there from the beginning to the end. He already knows what is going to happen before it happens; He gets us prepared and ready for our trials and tribulations.

On our way to the park one day, I bought my children some bubbles. I wanted to make the best out of that particular day because I was going through so much. I found myself in one situation after another where I felt like I was in quicksand, sinking slowly but surely with tons of brick weighing me down to make me sink even faster.

Inside I was crying out for help, and I wondered if God was listening. Simple situations turned into headaches because I had a lot on my mind. I was very upset with my children because they spilled the bubbles in the car and made a mess. I headed home, but I heard God say, "Turn the car around and go to the park." We got to the park, and we blew so many bubbles to the point where I did not know if we could blow any more. It shows God works in mysterious ways.

The bubbles were beautiful as we blew them into the air. Bubbles were everywhere: some bubbles formed clusters, some refused to float but quickly landed right on the ground, and a select few of them hovered beautifully in the air. God has a way of speaking to each of us, and He spoke to me through the bubbles.

I studied the bubbles as I blew them into the air one by one and also as I ran around in circles with many bubbles exploding at once. I identified with the single bubbles most because before I went to the park, I felt as though I were in the battlefield alone without armor or protection. However, when I saw the multitude of bubbles produced as I ran in the circle, I felt inner peace.

I started to smile as I received a message from God, "All the bubbles that are floating in the air are a sign to let you know you are never alone. I am always here during your battles and your lonely days."

I also heard Him say, "Those bubbles represent the many blessings I have in store for you; however, you must believe Me and cling onto My unchanging hand. Have I ever let you down? The single bubbles are the independent ones, they need my support, but they have faith that I will keep them afloat, but from time to time, individual bubbles will join a group of bubbles."

The bubbles in groups were not afraid to seek help, because we cannot go at everything alone. I felt as though God were saying, "The bubbles that landed on the ground lacked faith in Me." I looked at the bubbles as a life lesson to walk by faith and not by sight. We need to trust and believe that God is an on-time God at all times.

> For the word of the Lord is right and true; he is faithful in all He does. The Lord loves righteousness and justice; the earth is full of His unfailing love (Psalm 33:4-5).

Through the bubbles, God made what I thought was one of the worst days into the greatest conversation He and I had in a long while.

> My soul is weary with sorrow; strengthen me according to your word (Psalm 119:28).

God stepped in at the right time to show His grace was sufficient, and it renewed my strength. God reassured me that my troubles were taken care of. My children and I enjoyed ourselves that evening blowing bubbles until the sun set. That was one of the greatest moments in my life, a memory full of God's grace, peace, and joy.

I often spend time with my children individually to give them one on one time. "For God does not show favoritism" (Romans 2:11). One cloudy day, my daughter and I decided to take a stroll through the park. We had a great conversation and a good time bonding on the swings. I really enjoyed myself as I swung higher and higher, trying to touch the branch on a tree. As grown-ups, sometimes we have to take a moment to act like a child, full of laughter, joy, and believe in such things as a child would.

I had a good old time. I really felt like a kid and for that moment I did not have a lot on my mind, and I was free of stress. I felt at ease, cool, calmed, relaxed, as if I could jump off the swing and land in the white fluffy clouds. It was a wonderful feeling as my toes were getting massaged by the wind.

I looked up at the sky and saw God was forming different shapes with the clouds as they moved steady across the sky as the ocean's calm waves. While we were enjoying free falling on the swings, we noticed it started to sprinkle. My daughter and I continued to swing, hoping it would soon stop. I told her that if it started to rain harder then we would have to run to the car for shelter and find something else to do for our mommy and daughter day.

It started to rain harder and we were going to run for the car, but instead we continued to swing on the swings for awhile. Finally, we got off the swings and started dancing together in the rain.

> *May the God of hope fill you with all joy and peace as you trust in him, so that you may overflow with hope by the power of the Holy Spirit* (Romans 15:13).

At that moment in time I did not have any worries. What we thought was going to be a muddy evening sitting in traffic turned out to be the greatest time, full of laughter and showers of blessings.

The seasons started to change in my situation as well as the weather. My children were out of school for the summer, but my son was not old enough to watch his sibling while I went to work and school. I could not afford to send them to summer camp; however my youngest son's in-house sitter kept my oldest children while I went to school for a reasonable price. She helped me so much. For once I did not have to worry about the load I had on my shoulders, and I had the opportunity to focus on my classes.

My children and I made the best out of that summer. I might have been at my lowest with funds, but my children did not know it. Every Tuesday and Thursday we went to the movies because it was free movie day at the local theater, and the popcorn and slushies were one dollar.

I enrolled in a family fun summer package that offered free skating two days of the week and free bowling during the week for the entire summer. I could not afford to rent bowling shoes for all of us, but I searched online and found a great deal for some new bowling shoes for us all. God is so good!

We relaxed in the park nearly every day; we also had our weekly picnic there and took it easy. When I thought my funds were limited, God made the impossible possible. God blessed us with favor to have a wonderful and blessed summer.

The Lord will guide you always; He will satisfy your needs in a sun-scorched land and will strengthen your frame. You will be like a well-watered garden, like a spring whose waters never fail (Isaiah 58:11).

As I look back, I saw God turned that time into the greatest summer we could ever hope for.

As I shared in chapter 2, when my car was stolen it left me in a financial jam, but I continued to pray and ask God for His guidance. I remembered I always wanted a transitional car such as a mini-van to have more room for my up and coming business (Divergent S.P.E.E.D) because I did not have enough room for my equipment. Not only that, from time to time the thought came across my mind that my ex-husband's name was on our car that I paid off, and I felt as though we were still tied to each other.

I prayed and God said to me, "If I did not allow your car to be stolen, you would not have taken the chance to invest in a mini-van. Since the chains were broken, it was time to dispose of them for good. I knew you were strong enough to handle the challenge and suit up for the battle. Most importantly, your faith was strong enough to call on Me instead of cursing Me. Well done, My child, well done." I purchased a mini-van and do not have any more ties to my ex when it comes to material things.

However, I did not have the mini-van for long. My children and I went to an amusement park. My nieces came along as well, and we had a wonderful time, and afterwards we went to get something to eat. After we left the restaurant, a guy pulled out and hit my car full force. My family and I had to jump out of the car in the middle of the road. The air bags inflated and fluid was leaking from the vehicle.

I was thankful to see that everyone was safe and unharmed. I was taken back and I thought to myself, *Not again!* It was a long process, but I must say it turned out to be one of the greatest moments of my life because my family did not receive even a scratch.

My mini-van was giving me some issues and I ended up getting the SUV I always wanted, not to mention the fact that I only had to pay out of pocket twelve hundred dollars instead of over seven thousand dollars.

Now to Him Who is able to do immeasurably more than all we ask for imagine, according to His power that is at work within us (Ephesians 3:20).

Shortly after that, my daughter and I were having a mommy and daughter day. We got some breakfast, went to the movies, had some ice cream and were headed to get her hair done. After that, our plan was to get a massage, have dinner, and head home. However, that plan did not take place.

After getting some ice cream, I went to the ATM to get some money to pay her hairdresser. I had to use the restroom badly so I drove across the street to a restaurant to use the facilities there. Apparently I had dropped my wallet there but strangely, there was no one who saw it. I asked the manager if anyone turned in a purple wallet and the answer was no.

Time is everything because I was not in the restaurant for more than three minutes and my wallet was stolen. There were two men and a lady who looked suspicious. Everyone else in the restaurant was focused on their meal or whomever they were speaking to, but two men and a lady kept looking at my daughter and me as we walked back and forth to look for my wallet.

Since they kept staring, I asked them if they saw a purple wallet, and they started laughing and said no. I looked at them and honestly, they looked guilty. As we walked to the car, they were still looking at us. The lady was looking down as though she were looking through my wallet. I do not know for sure if they stole it, but my instinct was strong.

For the Lord gives wisdom; from His mouth come knowledge and understanding; He stores up sound wisdom for the upright; He is a shield to those who walk in integrity the paths of justice and watching over the way of His saints. Then you will understand righteousness and justice and equity, every good path; for wisdom will come into your heart, and knowledge will be pleasant to your soul; discretion will watch over you, understanding will guard you, delivering you from the way of evil,

*from men of perverted speech, who forsakes the paths of up-
rightness to walk in the ways of darkness, who rejoice in doing
evil and delight in the perverseness of evil, men whose path are
crooked and who are devious in their ways* (Proverbs 2:6-15).

While we were still looking for the wallet in the parking
lot, they continued to look at us. I called the police and my
daughter wrote down their license plate number, but the offi-
cers said it wasn't registered.

That wasn't the greatest moment of my life. I had that
wallet for over six years because when it was given to me, it
was one of the greatest moments of my life. A good friend of
mine, whom I call my sister, thought about me enough to
give it to me. When she purchased that wallet, I knew she
bought it with love and put in a lot of thought because it was
purple, and she knew that was my favorite color.

I remember when she gave me the wallet. We were in
Miami and she said with excitement, "Sis, I have a surprise
for you!" She was smiling from ear to ear. When I took it out
of the bag, it was a Coach purple wallet, with leather trim. It
was easy to carry because I was able to put it around my
wrist.

She said, "I noticed you carry around the same old red
wallet that you have had for years. I wanted to give you
something special since you are always helping people." I
loved it! I gave her a hug with tears in my eyes because it is
always a wonderful feeling to be thought of.

That was one of the greatest moments ever because not
too many people think of me to give me something. More
times than not they think of me to ask me for something. I
cherished that wallet because it was given to me out of love.

It saddens me to know there are so many distasteful

people in the world. I'm always aware of my surroundings;, but the incident it taught me a great lesson to always observe closely.

I'm sure after they went through my wallet they were highly disappointed because I had cancelled all my credit cards and did not have any cash. I am more than sure they threw my wallet away. Not only was I disappointed because they stole my wallet, but more so hurt because I can replace the credit cards, my license, and everything that was in my it, but the wallet was a gift that I could not replace. I felt violated because I work hard and earn everything I have. What a sad world we live in today.

We do not know why things happen the way they do, but we know God has it all worked out in advance. When we look back over a situation, we will see God redirected our path and turned what we thought was overwhelming into the greatest moments of our lives.

One of the greatest moments in my life is knowing that I've made a difference in someone's life for the better.

I love to teach. It is such a wonderful thing to partake in so many people's lives. In my class I have what I call, "Open Floor Discussion," which means we can talk about any and everything as long as we are respectful towards one another.

And let us consider how to stir up one another to love and good works, not neglecting to meet together, as is the habit of some, but encouraging one another, and all the more as you see the day drawing near (Hebrews 10: 24-25).

Not only did my students learn a lot from me, but I learned so much from them as well. It was a privilege to know my students put so much of their trust in me.

One day during Open Floor Discussion, one of my students asked me if I had seen my rating from a popular website. This website is where students rate professors and leave their comments. Basically, it helps future students decide whether they want to take a class with a particular teacher.

I decided to read the comments and I was surprised with what I read. My rating was a four point nine out of five stars and I had a hot chili pepper as a compliment. As I read the comments I became emotional because I really never knew how my students felt about me outside of class.

A couple comments stated, "Ms. Jackson always has a positive attitude, a bubbly smile, and most importantly she wants the best for all her students. She always says to turn the negative into a positive, and I do that every day because of Ms. J. I admire Ms. J's feedback and her communication. I love coming to her class because she is so much fun! We had to work hard in her class. Make sure you put your best foot forward because she expects the best from all her students. In my opinion we need more professors like Ms. J because she loves making a difference in people's lives. Ms. J helped me change my life around. Thank you!"

There were several comments that said, "Wow, Ms. J always has her past students come and sit in her class for the heck of it, just to hear her lectures. That is how interesting her class is. I look forward every day to going to Ms. J's class! Her class is so exciting, fun, and educating. I love Ms. J! Couldn't and wouldn't ask for a better professor!!"

Other comments would say, "Ms. J does not play about coming to class late, but she is a wonderful teacher who cares about her students and you can tell she loves her job."

I came across two or three comments that really touched

my heart, and tears formed in my eyes. One of the comments was: "Ms. Jackson is like no other person I've met. She is an outstanding, amazing, and wonderful person. When I took her class, she helped me look at life differently. She made me realize I do have something to live for and that I am someone. Ms. J helped me to love and put me first. I love Ms. J dearly. She is a remarkable blessing that God sent on time."

I had not known that I made a difference in so many people lives. I read about how many of my students really appreciate my being there to teach them for this season in their life.

And don't forget to do good and to share with those in need. These are the sacrifices that please God (Hebrews 13:16).

It is an honor to be used by God without any limitation or questions asked. One would think your greatest moments are only about you, but it is about the people who made a huge impact on your life as well.

I do not believe my greatest moments would have existed without being around the people whom I love or even being introduced to my lovely students who may not know that they made a huge impact in my life.

We have to learn how to let God use us according to His will because it's not only for someone else's benefit, but it is for our benefit as well. It is a life-changing event that might have turned your life around, given you that extra push, or done something as simple as put a smile on your face when you needed it the most. For sure, it will become one of the greatest moments that would not be forgotten.

God knows exactly how to make the best out of a moment and turn it into one of the greatest moments ever!

Dear Heavenly Father who repairs and replaces, we come together and thank You for the greatest moments of our lives. When we thought all else had failed, had been lost and destroyed, You knew in advanced the rugged road would soon come to an end. Most Gracious, walk with us and order our footsteps, lead us and use us according to Your will. Amen.

❧5❧

FATHER IS WITH ME

God is with us through our tribulation and He comforts us (2 Corinthians 1:3-4).

So many times in my life I have thought I received the short end of the stick. However, I had to believe that my Father was with me. When we fall short in our faith and life tackles us down, we need to fall straight on our knees and pray.

Submit yourselves, then, to God. Resist the devil, and he will flee from you (James 4:7)

When we pray we will feel our Father's presence, and we will know that our Father is with us.

On Thanksgiving Day, my husband (now my ex-husband) left to go visit his family out of town. I never thought in a million years he had the intention of not coming back. My older son was ten years old, my daughter was seven, and my youngest was eight months old. I remember that day clearly. He said that he was going up north to visit his family for the weekend, and I packed his clothes. For some unknown reason, I did not feel good about him leaving. At that time, our marriage was in jeopardy. I understood that he needed a break and peace of mind for a moment, but I never thought in my wildest dreams he would not return.

We had our issues just like any married couple. He recently had lost his job. I was going to school full time, taking care of my family by cooking, cleaning, washing, and being a supportive wife and mother. I guess that was not good enough.

Nevertheless, he was the breadwinner in our family. I was going to school to further my education so I too could bring money into the household. I understood why my husband thought that he had a lot on his plate, but being a wife, a mother, and a student, I had a lot on my plate too, but I was not willing to give up on my marriage.

Before my husband and I had gotten married, my grandmother told us, "If it gets too hot in the kitchen, take your butt to the back; and if it gets too hot in the back, then take your butt to the front." She also made it clear that we needed to keep our marriage issues private because outsiders and family could ruin a marriage. After going through the ups and downs in my marriage, I understand exactly what she meant.

After hearing my husband made it to his family's house safe and sound, I felt in my bones and knew in my heart that something was not right. We didn't speak to each other until one day I called him and I did not get an answer. When I called his mother's house phone, she made an excuse why he could not come to the phone. She had overstepped her boundaries and come between us in our marriage.

One day when I called, she told me that her son was not happy, and it was my fault as his wife and he would not be coming back. Right then and there I knew that I would have to fight for my marriage. His mother and I really never got along; she had the mindset that, since I was in school, I was not being a good wife, and that her son was the only one working to support our family. I thought the best interests for my family was for me to be a prayer warrior, supportive wife, a good mother to my children, and continue to get an education. That way, I could eventually help my husband by sharing the heavy financial load.

When I was younger, I lived next door to my grandparents. My siblings and I used to walk across the driveway, and my grandparents would have breakfast, snack, lunch, snacks, and dinner ready daily. My grandmother always took very good care of my grandfather. I remembered seeing her cooking, washing, and ironing my grandfather's clothes as he prepared himself for work.

My grandparents had structure in their home and worked together as a team. My grandparents led by example; when I was married I did what I was taught. My ex's mother always sheltered her sons. In my opinion she disabled her boys and made them weak. I always thought she never wanted her sons to have another woman in their lives. Furthermore, she never understood that she was hurting them as opposed to helping them.

A week passed and I still did not hear from my husband. I kept in contact with his cousin and he would transfer messages to me from my husband. Calling his cousin was the only way I could relay a message to him. I also kept in contact with his family, who resided in the same state. However, both of his cousins were married, and I knew that I could not continue to put my problems on his cousin's family. The calling ceased, and I had to hand my problems over to God because it was more than I could handle.

When my husband finally called, he told me that he was coming back, but he needed more time. I asked him how much time he needed because Thanksgiving break was over, our children were back in school, and the load was too heavy for me to bear. I told him whatever the problem was maybe we could work it out. I suggested that maybe we could go to counseling. However, he stated again he just needed more time. My emotions were uncontrollable. I was fed up, disappointed, tired, in pain, and hurt. After I tried to convince him to come home to make it work, he did not call for weeks.

A couple weeks passed and he still did not come home. I took a chance to call him and I was surprised he answered. I asked him numerous times if he could please come back to save our marriage, but he stated once again he was not ready. I begged him to come back so we could seek counseling; he said that it was not the right time. I did not know when I was going to hear from him again.

Before we got off the phone, I asked him if he could please come back to save our house. The house was in his name and was going into foreclosure. The only way for the house to be saved was if he came back to sign a document. I did not sign my name on the deeds because when we purchased the home, I did not think we were ready for a house. He said he would come down to sign the documents before the house went into foreclosure.

He did not come back to save the house, however, and it went into foreclosure. The letter from the bank told me I had two months to get my things together and move. I was thankful for the two months because Christmas was right around the corner. It was a blessing that my children and I would not be put out in the cold.

I prayed about the situation and asked God for His guidance. I missed a couple days of school because I did not have anyone to watch my eight-month-old son; I prayed about it, and I got online to find someone nearby to watch him. I had to go to school because that was the only income I had coming in. I had a work-study position, and something was better than nothing.

God blessed me to find an in-house daycare that was down the street from our house. I did not want to leave my son with a complete stranger, but I had faith that God was with my son as I took my oldest children to school and headed to school myself.

> He replied, "Truly I tell you, if you have faith as a small as a mustard seed, you can say to this mountain, 'Move from here to there,' and it will move. Nothing will be impossible for you" (Matthew 17:20).

God sent the in-house babysitter into my life for a reason. I told her about my situation, and it turned out she was going through something similar. The price was reasonable. I knew right then and there, my Father was with me, working behind the scenes in my favor.

Every day I was in pain, hurting, and tired; I was angry because I felt like I had the weight of the world on my shoulders. I was filled with so much sorrow; I never thought it was possible to feel so many emotions all at once. My younger children never knew I was struggling, but I knew my oldest one had a clue.

I did not show any emotions around them. I never cried in front of my children. I also never showed any weakness to my family or friends. I always put on a strong face because I did not want anyone to worry or feel any satisfaction that I was going through hard times. Some people love to see you down and out, facing challenges, because misery loves company, but I refused to show any signs of weakness in public. When I was alone, I cried and fell on my knees, asking God to help me, and instantly I felt His presence near.

Take my yoke upon you and learn from me, for I am gentle and humble in heart, and you will find rest for your souls (Matthew 11:29).

I heard God say, "You will get through this, My child; I am taking you around the long way. That way, you will be able to take a break here and there. You will be able to hear Me clearer, and soon you will gain more strength than you ever imagined." I did not understand it at the time, but I had no doubt my Father was with me.

I could not believe how fast Christmas came around, and my husband was still up north. At that point I knew then he was not coming back. I spoke to him but not on a daily basis because it was stressful speaking to him without his support and assistance. He took the easy road, living up north, staying warm, eating hot chili, and living with his mother. I was the one stressed, worried about how our utilities were going to stay on, how I was going to get diapers for my little one, and all there is to do in order to take care of my children.

I was clinging to the hope that our marriage was going to be saved. Little did I know at the time, but he did not care and did not have any remorse about his family barely surviving.

At my first defense, no one came to my support, but everyone deserted me. May it not be held against them. But the Lord stood at my side and gave me strength, so that through me the message might be fully proclaimed and all the Gentiles might hear it. And I was delivered from the lion's mouth. The Lord will rescue me from every evil attack and will bring me safely to his heavenly kingdom. To him be the glory for ever and ever. Amen (2 Timothy 16-18).

I did not have any money to buy Christmas gifts so I went to different church events to get my children a couple gifts. I did not know for sure if my husband would be back before Christmas or on Christmas day, and one of the churches was giving out packs of socks and t-shirts, and I got him a pack of each.

When my children awakened on Christmas morning, they were filled with excitement and happy with the gifts they were given. Seeing my children with smiles on their faces was my Christmas gift. For the first time in a long time I had peace of mind and joy in my heart. We had a great Christmas, thanks to God.

I thought the worst was over and I did not expect what was to come. When my husband left, I thought we were caught up on our bills; however, I was wrong. After I dropped my children off at school, I encountered a traffic roadblock. When the police officer checked my driver's license, car insurance, and registration, I did not know that my car insurance had lapsed.

I had my youngest son in the car and I asked the officer, "Is there a way I can call someone to come pick up my baby?" Since I did not have insurance, I thought that he was going to lock me up. I tried to stay strong, but I broke down and positioned myself for him to put handcuffs on me.

I cried and I said to the officer, "I do not think that my life could be any worse." I gave him a description of what happened to me in the previous couple weeks. I told him that my husband left me with three children, I had been to different churches to get food and clothing, I'd been to two different organization to receive help with paying my bills, and I just did not know what to do. The only thing I could do was to fall on my knees, cry, and ask God to help me.

I knew right then and there my Father was with me every step of the way. I felt my Father rock me in the cradle of His arms. I felt His presence. I heard His voice saying everything would be okay.

The officer asked me to follow him. I asked him where were we going and he said, "I am going to take you to a place so you can get insurance on your car." When I told the officer, "I do not have any money," he said he was paying for the first month for me, and if necessary, the down payment.

Now to him who is able to do immeasurably more than all we asked or imagine, according to his power that is at work within us (Ephesians 3:20).

I knew that it was nobody but God, my Father in heaven who touched the officer's heart and blessed me to have car insurance. My Father was with me!

A few days later, my children and I had a long day. I bought some groceries and headed home to make a warm, healthy, hearty dinner. I was exhausted and tired; I remember that day clearly. I struggled taking my little one into the house. It was very cold outside; he was asleep and I did not want to wake him or get him out of his car seat. When I opened the door, the house was freezing. I flipped the switch and the lights had been cut off.

I fell on my knees asking God, "How much more do You want me to bear?" I told my daughter and my son to stand by the door with their baby brother because I had to gather their clothes in the dark for school the next day.

I could hardly see a thing; the only light I had was the

street lights. I gathered my children's things, drove to my mother's house, and stayed for the night. Needless to say, it was a restless night because it was nothing like sleeping in my own bed, but it was a blessing to have somewhere for my children and me to sleep.

The next day, I called around to see if anyone was lending assistance with utility bills; however almost everyone I called said they had already run out of funds. When I finally received a yes, I had to bring them the utility bills. In the end I was told they could not assist me because my name was not on the bills. (The utility bills were in my husband's name.) I tried explaining the situation to them; however, they had to follow the proper protocol, which I understood.

I took a chance and went from church to church, until God directed me to the right one after I had been calling around for hours. They understood my situation, prayed for me, and wrote a check in the company's name. I took the check to the electricity company and my lights were turned back on the same day.

After the bill was paid, I went home to turn on the heat; afterwards, I picked my children up from school. When we got home the house was so cozy and toasty. I cooked a healthy dinner and I helped my children with their homework and gave them a warm relaxing bath. After we had our devotions, we all enjoyed a peaceful night of rest.

I knew that my Father was with me every step of the way because He blessed me instantly to have my electricity bill paid and turned on the same day. I could not thank God enough for touching so many people to help me and my children.

When we find ourselves in a tough situation, we do not need to panic or worry; instead we need to look up because that is where our help comes from. I am only human, however, I realized during my toughest times I developed a closer relationship with God. I did not have anyone to turn to—no one but God.

I remembered helping so many people in their tough times, but when I asked them for help, either they did not answer or if they did, their answer was, "I'm sorry, but I do not have it." In my battles, I thought I was all alone, but God revealed Himself through so many strangers who were kind enough to help my children and me.

I knew that during my hardship and trying time, I could not worry because it was beyond my means. I knew I had to let go and let God. I was weak, but my Father was strong.

But he said to me, "My grace is sufficient for you, for my power is made perfected in weakness." Therefore I will boast all of the gladly about my weakness, so that Christ's power may rest on me (2 Corinthians 12:9).

I knew I could not show any sign of weakness to my children or other people because I did not want them to see my suffering. When I was alone it was okay to talk to God and show Him my weakness, for I knew that He was the only One who understood. During my weakest times, God hugged me and cradled me in His arms because I was and still am His child.

God was the only One I could trust, and I knew He did not celebrate during my trials; instead, He renewed my strength to carry on. Later that night, I could not thank God enough for directing my path and for the strength He gave me. Every day, I was going through something new, every day God was with me, and every day God gave me the strength to carry my cross.

Two days before Christmas, we were all excited. During the Christmas season I always take my children to a particular house that always has bright lights and the owners of the house always dress up as Mr. and Mrs. Santa Claus. My children were so happy. They took pictures, enjoyed the lights, and had a great time.

Sometimes in life we can have the worst days, but when you grab hold of your faith and know how powerful God is, He will be with you, He will carry you, and He will comfort you by letting you know everything will work out. God can change every situation; you just have to have faith to know that God is able. I know that my Father is with me every step of the way because He has always kept His promises and He hasn't failed me yet.

When we go through our trials and tribulation in life, we need to remember God is the Lily of the Valley. He is Alpha and Omega, and He always has the first and last word. We cannot be afraid of what man may think or do to us. God loves us so much that He gave His only begotten Son to bear the cross for our sins.

We have to keep the faith, know that God is able and know that God will fight our battles for us.

We are hard pressed on every side, but not crushed; perplexed, but not in despair; persecuted, but not abandoned; struck down, but not destroyed (2 Corinthians 4:8-9).

Sometimes we may feel like our Father is nowhere to be found; however, He is in the midst of our trials, giving us the strength to bear the cross in order for us to earn a crown.

Dear Heavenly Father of Victory,

Thank You for Your unchanging undivided love in both good and difficult times. When my enemies try to shatter my light and leave me in darkness, they failed to realize Your light is the only light that is sufficient. I am more than thankful for every cross I have to carry because I know that You are with me every second and every step of the way. When I thought I did not have anything else to give, thank You for Your grace and for not giving up on me. Amen.

❧6❧

GIFT OF TEARS

Jesus answered her, if you knew the gift of God and who it is that asks you for a drink, you would have asked him and he would have given you living water (John 4:10).

The gift of tears does not include only tears of sorrow, but tears of joy as well. Tears represent courage, faith, hope, and vison. They are a result of rising above your limitations from unexpected obstacles. However, if we did not have interference, we would not be able to develop a relationship with God to help us grow and prosper.

When I graduated and earned my bachelor's degree, I cried tears of joy because so many people were waiting for me to fail. I remembered my financial aid advisor even told me I should change my major because my classes were so challenging.

There were family members who told me they came to my graduation because they had to see with their own eyes that I was graduating. They did not believe I was going to school, working, and raising three children alone. They failed to realize that those challenges were in God's plan, and they were the process of God forming my foundation.

Not much comes easily; and if it does, be prepared to lose it. Nothing is given; it is earned. Something that is worth having should not be questioned nor should it come to us easily; what is valuable should be worth the challenge and difficult times. After all, something worth having produces growth and a firm foundation to stand on.

I heard people say, "She will not graduate with three kids, because she has been in college forever." I might have been an undergraduate for a mighty long time; however, during those trying times, there were rules and regulations I had to follow in order for God to reveal to me the gift of hard working tears. There were protocols I had to follow while carrying my cross in order for me to earn my crown.

The procedures were not the easiest tasks to complete, but afterwards the gift of tears healed each wound caused by negative words and doubts from others. Through it all, God was there with me to seal the foundations that were cracked by my shaking faith. Once my foundation was sealed, God gave me the strength to build perseverance and endurance to complete and execute each obstacle that was set before me.

Therefore, since we have been justified through faith, we have peace with God through our Lord Jesus Christ, through whom we have gained access by faith into this grace in which we now stand. And we boast in the hope of the glory of God. Not only so, but we also glory in our sufferings, because we know that suffering produces perseverance; perseverance, character; and character, hope. And hope does not put us to shame, because God's love has been poured out into our hearts through the Holy Spirit, who has been given to us (Romans 5:1-5).

By God's grace, strength, and mercy, I walked across the stage and turned my tassel with pride as my children watched their mother graduate from college. I felt like an eagle soaring high.

I am more than sure many people thought I was crying

tears of joy because I graduated from college. God knew why I was crying, and it was more than tears of joy. The gifts God blessed me with were faith that couldn't be demolished; hope knowing that the days ahead were going to be better than the days before; and courage to know if I kept jumping a little higher, I would be able to jump over each hurdle without falling.

God was with me every step of the way during my journey, and for that I will be forever grateful. It was a long journey, but as I look back at my struggles, I see it was worth the trials and tribulations I had to face. It taught me how to fight and not give up, and most importantly, it made me a new and better person.

The gift of tears will have a person look at life in a totally different aspect. As for me, I think differently at what comes my way. Not letting fear strike me, I strike against fear by knowing there is always a way to solve a solution. The key is that we have to take time to figure it out instead of letting negative thoughts take over and cloud our mind. When they do, we worry and worrying turns into stress. Nothing good comes from discouragement but sickness.

I learned that my tears made me change my life statement to: "With God I can and I will." I was not going to let what someone did or said to me change my frame of thinking. I did not have the option to quit or let life's complications get the best of me. I refused to continue to trip over hurdles that I knew I could jump over. I had to ask God to give me a tad bit more height, strength, determination, and endurance to complete this journey.

God renewed my strength so many times when I had to sacrifice so much. So many years I had spent studying during the midnight hours while my children were resting. I tried to stay ahead in my studies as I waited in line in the freezing cold to seek assistance with paying my utility bills, catching up on homework because I had to take classes in order to receive assistance with my mortgage.

He was there with me as I was multi-tasking, helping my children with their homework while I cooked and completed my homework. I attended two schools at one time, taking three classes at one school and four classes at the other for an entire year while continuing to work as a work-study student. God and I were the only two who knew how many sacrifices I made while trying to complete my undergraduate studies.

> *But for those who hope in the Lord will renew their strength. They will soar on wings like eagles; they will run and not grow weary, they will walk and not be faint* (Isaiah 40:31).

Many people never knew what I was going through because I never showed any signs of stress. I cried during my most tired and weakest point only when no one was around. I never told anyone because I didn't think they would understand. I knew the only advice they would have given me would have been negative. I couldn't let anybody or anything sidetrack my thinking. Sometimes I kept away from my family and some friends because I couldn't afford to be distracted. I had to keep my mind steadfast on God.

> *But when you fast, anoint your head and wash your face that your fasting may not be seen by others but your Father who is in secret. And your Father who sees in secret will reward you* (Matthew 6: 17-18).

When I was walking up the steps to be acknowledged, I looked at my children smiling as my eyes were filled with gifts of indescribable joy. My oldest son was eleven, my daughter was eight, and my little one was one years old. I looked down at them and I turned my tassel.

After I shook the president's hand and walked down the steps I said, "God, WE did it!" What a day of joy racing all over my body after so many obstacles I had to face head on. I am highly favored and truly blessed that I did not have to take my journey alone.

There were times when God said, "I am not going to take you *through* it; instead I am going to take you *around* it." Going around might have taken me a lot longer than going through, but as God took me around my trials and tribulations, I had more time to talk and walk with God. He gave me the opportunity to rest in Him when I became weary. He assured me that when I was dehydrated, I would no longer thirst because He was my fountain of life and truth.

Everyone who drinks this water will be thirsty again, but whoever drinks the water I give them will never thirst. Indeed, the water I give them will become in them a spring of water welling up to external life (John 4:13-14).

Going around might have taken longer than expected, but I had more time to think because God was my peace and my joy. When things are taking longer than you think they should, do not get discouraged. We have to let God take us around our trials and tribulations. Sometimes going around gives us more time to spend with God. We will be able to hear God clearly, take a break, and we will be more rested to fight our battles.

When we go through, it is similar to taking a short cut, instead of going the longer route. When taking the longer route and going around, we have more time to think, but going straight through is totally different because we are rushing, instead of taking our time to make wise decisions.

God knows exactly what He is doing; sometimes it is better to go around it, as opposed to going through it. We will have gained a better understanding and a better view. Most importantly, we will find rest in Him and we will become closer to our Father.

Although it wasn't easy, I accomplished each challenge. I fought a good fight on the battlefield, I prayed every waking day. It was hard work, but I was not alone for God was with me every step of the way.

Let us not become weary in doing good, for at the proper time we will reap a harvest if we do not give up (Galatians 6:9).

Do not give up when God takes you around. Hold steadfast; let Him use you. It is a wonderful feeling to cry the gift of tears and joy. It forms an unbreakable bond and unconditional love only you and God will understand.

Tears are transformational and they broaden your view. After I earned my bachelors in Biology, I asked God, "What's next?"

Trust in the Lord with all your heart, and do not lean on your own understanding. In all your ways acknowledge Him, and He will straight your plans (Proverbs 3:5-6).

I never thought about attending graduate school until one day when I came across a certain lady. She and I were waiting in line to check out. I just came from yoga class and she asked me how I stayed in shape. I started to talk about my exercise and nutritional plan. After having a healthy conversation later that day, I decided to apply for graduate school for a master's degree in Exercise Science.

I enjoyed graduate school. I met so many wonderful people. My professors always wanted the best for their students. One professor stood out the most to me; he was the best professor that I ever had. I took his Upper and Lower Extremity class. His class was challenging with the paper and pencil task, but I learned so much there. He was an awesome professor. We keep in touch until this day.

I must say that I loved graduate school more so than my undergraduate studies. Maybe it was because in undergraduate school, we had to take so many unnecessary classes. In graduate school we jumped right into the classes that were required for the degree.

After I completed my classes, practicum/intern, and graduated with my master's degree, I encounter bad news from the financial aid department that prevented them from releasing my degree and transcripts. I was treated unfairly due to their mistakes. I filed a case against them, and my back up plan was to apply to another graduate program.

I was accepted and graduated with my second master's degree in Healthcare Administration/Health Science. I learned through my trials and tribulations from the past that I always must have a plan from A-Z. If those plans don't work out, then I have to start on the number scale of 1 through a trillion if necessary.

The heart of man plans his way, but the Lord establishes his steps (Proverbs 16:9).

Faith, persistence, and determination are always a win-win combination.

I never thought in a million years I would earn two master's degrees and be working on my PhD. God paved the way for me, whether if it's going through it or going around it. Either way, we should let God lead us down the path He paved for us. God wants us to believe in Him and know that He has it all covered. We have to suit up for the challenge and know that He is able.

Through years of tough times, many tears have fallen from my eyes; I learned how to count every tear that fell down my cheeks as a gift of joy. Every tear I cried restored my soul, refreshed my spirit, cleansed my thoughts, and washed the residue so I could clearly see the path that was in front of me.

I planted, Apollos watered, but God gave the growth (1 Corinthians 3:6).

My tears gave me strength and courage to know that within time, everything will fall into place for my good.

When we are fragile, He shows us mercy and gives us extra security. God heals the hurt and the wounded with His tender care and love until the scar does not exist. He begins to work on us very patiently to open up our heart from disappointment and resentment to turn them into something that we thought would not ever occur again—unconditional love to be able to give and love freely without fear.

For still the vision awaits its appointed time; it hastens to the end—it will not lie. If it seems slow, wait for it; it will surely come; it will not delay (Habakkuk 2:3).

My tears gave me the strength to turn hurt into forgiveness, and forgiveness into love. Tears are extraordinary showers that are filled with a purpose. Whether they are tears of sorrow or tears of joy, God is there to wipe away every one.

Because the Lamb who is at the center of the throne will shepherd them; He will guide them to springs of living waters, and

God will wipe away every tear from their eyes (Revelation 7:17).

God works in mysterious ways, and He is simply amazing. I know that I do not deserve His love and all the bountiful blessings He has given me. I know God loves me so much because He does not look at my flaws like man would. Instead, He works with me in ways I could not ever imagine to make me a better person.

Tears are a blessing,. They give us an opportunity to look back at the obstacles and challenges we faced and see them turned into triumph.

Has God answered your cry? Think about His goodness and how He has turned your life around for good, even when you questioned His final decision.

Renewed strength and living water that runs through my soul, please continue to wash away any negative energy that consumes my mind and train of thinking; thank You for quenching my thirst when my soul is dehydrated, brittle, and weak; cleanse me Father as You see fit, according to Your will. Amen.

❧ 7 ❧

CALMING THE STORM

We have peace with God through our Lord Jesus Christ (Romans 5:1).

Giving your life to Christ does not mean you will not have trials or live a life of freedom without a journey to conquer. When you give your life to Christ, you are considered a soldier of the Lord. You should always have on your protective gear, your armor, because the trials you face head on will help you to gain trust in God.

Faith gives us strength and steady peace more than we can ever know during tribulations and difficult times. Feelings of discouragement, complications, frustration, and doubt are a part of life because we are human. When our situation in life gets us in that state of mind of negative thinking, we should talk to God to soothe our mind and meditate on His Word.

Have you ever thought that maybe God leads us into troubled waters so we can learn to cling to Him and trust in Him? Many times the raging water tried to sink me and drown my faith. God was my life jacket; He was there to keep my head above the troubled raging waters.

Wait for the Lord; be strong and take heart and wait for the Lord (Psalm 27:14).

As my faith continues to grow stronger and stronger each day, I continue to learn; sometimes it takes looking back on the situation before we can see how our faith has grown.

Plenty of times I felt I was backed up into a corner without anywhere to go. The only action I could take was to pray for serenity, peace, and strength. No matter what I did, at times it still was not enough for my children, family, and friends. They did not know everything I was going through, although they knew enough. I felt it was a selfish act of ignoring my needs. They were more focused on their own needs and what I could do for them. They did not understand the pressure I was under because in their eyes I was superwoman.

Their perspective of me is, "She has strength, she is not hurting for anything, she is always happy, she never has any worries, she can help us, and she is just fine." They neglected to see I am human. I cannot do it all. I might at times have made it look easy, but it is not easy. God's grace and mercy were the only reasons I was able keep pushing and moving on.

God always calms the raging storm at the right time because He knows how much we can bear. During the quiet and raging waves, I read over my journals; they made me smile, cry, and also had me wondering and thanking God for being so good to me. After reading my journals, I meditated on God's goodness. I felt His peace when He walked with me, cried with me, and cradled me to give me rest, even when I felt all alone and overwhelmed.

In the midst of the raging storm, God calmed it right on time, such as when I was searching high and low numerous times to pay my bills, and I asked my family and some of my friends to help if they could, but they would say that they didn't have it. What frustrated me the most was that the same people I had helped could never help me in return. That was okay because I knew my God would not fail me; He is always an on-time God.

He would either direct me to the right place to receive help with an assistance program, have my paycheck come a day or two early, or my refund from school be right on time. As the years went on and if I was able to, I would pay my bills three months in advance so I knew my children and I would have shelter, lights, water, and gas for those months.

God calmed the storm right on time when life tackled me down with despair and sorrow. When I felt I was in sinking sand, God pulled me out just in time. I remembered when I was in an Endocrinology class, taking a quiz. I received a call from my mother-in-law. I did not take the first call, but when she called me back-to-back I walked out of class to answer the phone. She called me to tell me my husband was contemplating committing suicide. He was at home, calling everyone and saying he was going to kill himself because the company he was working for decided to let him go.

That itself was too much to take in at once, but she made it worse by blaming me for his thoughts since I was in school getting an education to better my family life in the long run. She kept screaming, "It is your fault; all he does is work, work, and work, while you are in school!" As she was yelling and screaming, I felt as though the storm turned into a tsunami because she made it clear that if he killed himself, I should always remember that it was my fault. The storm was getting completely out of control as she brutally tortured me in the conversation. Only God knew what I was going through. (My husband always felt as though he could not make a move without her permission.)

I could have easily lashed out at her and blamed her because she was the one who insisted that he should take the district manager position for the company. I asked him not to take the position because being a property manager over two properties was stressful enough. When he was the property manager, my children and I were the ones who were in the office day in and night. We were the ones sacrificing sleep, but we understood and we were supportive.

Since we used to stay so late in the office, we brought our children's blankets, television, and VHS so they could watch movies, and we stored food in the refrigerator. We also purchased an air mattress so they would be comfortable sleeping, just in case we were in the office overnight and they had to go to school the next morning. His mother did not know half of what our family went through. Nearly every day we were in the office faithfully, even on Sundays after church.

His mother only thought she knew what was going on. She wanted him to take the district manager position because she was greedy and thinking about money. His mother was not looking out for her son's best interest; she was not thinking about the emotional and physical stress he and his family would have to endure. She was only thinking about the increase in his salary and how she was going to benefit from his earnings. Unlike her, I knew how accepting this position would affect him and our family, and that is why I asked him to decline the offer.

After he told his mother I suggested he should not take the position, she called me and gave me an earful. She yelled, "You want to keep him down; you do not want him to get ahead while you are going to school to be a doctor so you can leave him when you complete school!"

I wanted to tell her that is not how medical school works. I was still in undergraduate school, and if I had followed through on my thoughts of becoming a doctor, I had to attend four years of medical school, not to mention take specialized classes in the field where I chose to practice. I had to get accepted into an intern program, and I would have to attend more than a couple years in the program. I would also have to pass the Medical Boards, apply and get accepted into a residency program, work for a couple years, and then hopefully become an attendant in a hospital.

That is more than ten years of hard work of schooling, studying, and practicing, not to mention still caring for my husband and children. Does that sound like I had time to plot to leave my husband because I was going to school?

People who do not educate themselves are sometimes quick to judge, without knowing all the facts. I would not have left him; I would have made life easier for our family.

When I pulled in the driveway, I ran into the house. My husband was lying on the floor crying, with his Bible opened. I consoled him and reminded him the children and I loved him and that we needed him alive and well.

The storm that was once a tsunami was filled with dark skies, and gusty winds, and the sand tried to block my view, but God calmed the storm.

Days went by, hard days, in which not only did I have to care for my children, I had to be on the lookout to make sure my husband was safe and his thoughts were positive. I kept up my normal routine; however I added more to the mix and made time to send about twenty of my husband's resumes off in the mail. On Tuesdays and Thursdays I went to my mother's job to fax off his resumes as well. I was working overtime, far and beyond. I prayed for a peace of mind and strength. Every time the storms got out of hand, God was always there at the right time to calm the storm.

In the midst of the raging storm, God calmed it right on time when my husband left to stay with a friend for a while. I remember that night, my little one was crying. I was tired from moving around all day. I was the one taking the kids and picking them up from school, making trips to my mother's job sending off my husband's resume, taking care of my little one, going to school myself, cooking, cleaning, and trying to keep peace in my home.

The storm was calm during the day; however, it would rage after I returned home from a long day to a smelly, musty house to see my husband lying on the floor huffing over the Bible in distress.

Later that night, after I fell asleep, my little one started crying. At that time he was five months old. I did not have the energy to move. I asked my husband to pick him up, change, and feed him. He let him lie there and cry. After I got up, that is when he got up. I was mad and I hit him on his leg and said, "I have it!" I did not strike him in a disrespectful way. That is when my husband called his mother, stormed out of the house, and left.

His mother tells the story that I put hands on him and beat him around the house. I did not have the time or energy to argue with her, let alone beat anyone because I was beyond being exhausted. I had to focus on my son. When I settled him down, I tried to rest because I knew I soon had to tackle the long day that was ahead of me.

During the early morning hours around three a.m., I finally fell asleep. I did not get enough rest because I had to get up at five thirty in the morning. I had to make the best out of the day.

Since my husband stayed at his friend's house, which was near the children's school, I asked him if he could he pick up the kids, and I would pick them up after I left school. I was surprised he agreed.

On the days I did not go to school, I would cook a healthy, hearty meal, and take it to my husband when I picked the kids up from his friend's house. I think about that from time to time and ask myself why I did that. I always come up with the same answer. I did it out of love.

The storm would rage when I asked him to come back home because I needed help during the middle of the night with our little one and with the responsibilities around the house since he wasn't working. He would tell me he was not ready to come back home. I was angry because I felt it was not fair for him to sit over at his friend's house and play video games all day as if he did not have any responsibilities at home. He came back home to tell me he was going to visit his family up north for Thanksgiving, and as I mentioned before, after he left, he did not come back.

When the storm raged out of control, I was under much pressure not having anywhere to live with my three children after the house went into foreclosure. God stepped in right on time and I was approved to move into an income based apartment. The area might not have been the safest, but I did not have to go back to my mother's house. That was a blessing in itself.

During the time I stayed in the apartment, I became

overwhelmed with stress because I had so much going on and did not know how to handle the load. God calmed the storm right on time when I was in my closet crying and pleading to Him for His mercy and grace because I didn't know which way to turn.

He is always wrestling in prayer for you, that you may stand firm in all the will of God, mature and fully assured (Colossians 4:12).

I felt as though I were going to lose my mind. Never before had I encountered so much agony, pain, and torture at the same time. It was hard to act the role I was given. When I was at school, work, around my family, friends, and children, I was forced to smile. I did not have a choice but to smile or I was going to break down mentally, physically, and emotionally. I could only express my feelings when I was alone, which was not often.

One sunny Saturday morning, I finally broke down because I did not have the strength to put on a fake smile. I balled myself up in my closet with the lights off and pleaded with God. I cried and asked Him to shed His mercy on me. I needed more than strength; I needed to be rejuvenated. I needed more than peace; I needed to take back what the enemy had stolen from me. I needed more than ambition to sweep away the tower that my enemies shattered. I needed God's wisdom and power to help me with the wrecking ball to tear down the remains of what was left so He could polish up my foundation and help me build a new tower.

I needed to reconstruct my thoughts; to shed the dry, brittle, and dead skin. I needed to be revived and hydrated. I was tired of making it easy for Satan. The only way to stop him was to calm my nerves, stop pretending to the outside world, and call on God for help. The only way out was to ask God to wash me whole. I thought that clearly it would be enough evidence and create a new me.

After I cried out to the Lord, He eased and calmed the storm. He had my grandmother call me right on time. She said, "I am trying to cook my sweet potatoes, and God kept telling me to call you. I told him I will call my baby girl in a little while, but He said, 'No, call her right now.' So here I am calling you."

My grandmother's voice changed; out of nowhere she had so much authority as though God were speaking through her. She said, "God told me to tell you to let it go, pick up your cross, and carry it." After her voice returned to normal she said, "Now I have to get back to cooking my sweet potatoes, and I will call you and check on you later."

After I received the message, I sat there for a while. I wiped my face, stood up and as I was about to walk out of my closet, I heard God say, "Thank You for trusting in Me and for not underestimating Me because I can shake the mountains without anyone feeling it, and I can make an explosion without a sound being heard."

When I walked out of my closet, I said, "God I am ready." I took up my cross, the cracks in my foundation were sealed, and my foundation was polished and renewed. I was ready to partake in building a strong tower; I asked God to lead the way as I followed.

God calmed the raging storm right on time when I had to have knee surgery for the third time. My caseworker from my income-based insurance was heartless. She told me less than fourteen hours before my surgery that I had to reschedule. I explained to her the doctor's office was closed and I had to be at the hospital at six a.m. the next morning. She did not have a care in the world when she said, "You can call them tomorrow and let them know you do not have insurance and you have to reschedule." I tried explaining to her that I already had put in my two weeks' notice and my supervisor already found someone to cover my classes. She said, "Ms. Jackson, well, that is not my problem, I will not be able to help you, and you can take it for what it is."

I knew God was not going to disappoint me.

I am the Lord your God who takes hold of your right hand and says to you, Do not fear; I will help you (Isaiah 41:13).

If my insurance was not going to be approved I would accept it as God's will. God told me to call a former caseworker who could assist me; however, she did not work for the county I received my benefits from. She looked over my case and she stated, "I do not understand why your case worker cannot adjust your insurance."

I was told I did not turn in my last check stub, but I had. However, according to the college and their school-calendar schedule, we did not get paid for the month of August. I tried to explain; however, that was not good enough. I had to call my supervisor and within ten minutes she wrote a letter explaining how the payroll worked, and she sent a copy of the rules and regulations of how payments are set up for the year. My former caseworker suggested I should send it to my caseworker as soon as possible.

I forwarded the documents to my caseworker. She did not respond, so my former caseworker contacted her supervisor and her superior gave her permission to process and take the necessary steps to approve my insurance. Sadly, the only steps my caseworker had to take were to hit the approval button.

My insurance was squared away and I rested well that evening to prepare for my surgery. When I think about the situation, what is unbelievable is that my caseworker was supposed to help me—that was her job. It is amazing to see how some people judge you because of your current situation. I believe since I was receiving government assistance she thought I was worthless and sat on my butt daily. Once again, God stepped in right on time and sent an angel to approve my insurance less than a day before my surgery. By God's grace, it was a successful surgery.

Sometimes I felt as though I were going to lose my mind because I had to do this and that, be here and there, as if I were not just one person. I remembered one day clearly, I was driving and said, "Lord, I am beyond stressed, and I do not know where to go or which way to turn. I need comfort and a peace of mind." I heard Him clearly; I received an immediate response. He said, "Come to me." I started to cry, and I said, "Where, Lord, where do You want me to go." He said, "My voice is made of many waters and you can hear Me clearly. Come to the water."

My heart has heard you say, "Come and talk with me." And my heart responds, "Lord, I am coming" (Psalm 27:8).

My children thought I was playing around, because when I got home I packed my bags, anointed my forehead, and washed my face. Only God knew I was fasting. I called my cousin and asked her to pick up the kids and I got in my car and went to the beach. I did not call to make a reservation; I just got on the road and trusted God. I did not listen to the radio or talk on the phone. I was at peace because I talked to God the entire time while I was driving.

When I arrived at my destination, I went to the hotel where I normally stayed with my children; it was four hundred dollars for the weekend. I could not afford it, but I said, "Lord I am here and I am going to trust in You." I swiped my card, went up to my room, opened the sliding door, and heard God's voice while the waves were playing a tune.

The entire time I fasted, wrote in my book, and listened to God as He spoke to me. I stayed in my room with the sliding door open during my entire stay. I had a sense of peace spiritually, emotionally, and physically.

Finally, my mind was at rest and I enjoyed spending alone time with God. Although it took five hours getting there and going back home, that was the best combined ten hours of my life. Sometimes, we have to step out in faith and listen to God.

When we feel as though the storm will never let up, we have to let God be our shelter. Give it to God and know He will calm the storm.

"For my thoughts are not your thoughts, neither are your ways my ways," *declares the Lord* (Isaiah 55:8).

We have to keep in mind that God already sees and knows the outcome before He calms the storm. He wants to see how long it will take for us to call on Him. If we called on Him, He wants to see how long we are going to keep the faith and know that He is faithful. He will never disappoint us; He always and forever will be an on-time God.

Keep in mind that God will calm the storm right on time when we feel attacked when people and life circumstances try to break our spirit. We have to let go and let God provide us with a solution. He will calm the storm right on time The current of the water is never too strong to open our hearts and lives to deepen our faith. We must be willing to receive and expect God's renewed strength. We have to be strong enough to expect the blessings God has prepared for us.

When I thought all was lost, God, You were always there on time to ease the storms that were raging in my life. It is amazing to see how the sea obeys Your command. Your hands control the waves in my life, and when I feel unsettled, You are always there to be my Shield and my Shelter. Thank You for being the Storm Calmer and my Covenant when the storm is beyond my control. Amen.

❧ 8 ❧

FACING THE IMPOSSIBLE

What is impossible with man is possible with God (Luke 18:27).

At times we are faced with challenges that seem to be impossible to meet, but when you fall on your knees and ask God for help, the impossible turns into the possible. I have met many challenges I thought were impossible, but when I asked God for guidance, I had to suit up to fight more battles in His strength.

When I was going through one of the toughest times in my life, I thought I had to place college on hold because I had so much on my plate.

After I finally found an in-home daycare for my baby, I was approved by a non-profit organization receive assistance with my bills for the month. I thought I was finally coming up for a breath of fresh air until I received a letter in the mail stating I lost my financial aid because I did not meet the requirements.

My heart dropped because I worked so hard to get everything in order so I could go to school and focus on my studies. Putting school on hold was not an option for me. In order for me to find a reliable job to care for my family, I had to graduate from college. I walked into my room, locked my door, sat in my closet, and had a pity party for about thirty minutes. After my pity party, I found myself in a moment of silence.

> *He who dwells in the shelter of the Most High will abide in the shadow of the Almighty. I will say to the Lord, "My refuge and my fortress, my God, in whom I trust." "For He will deliver you from the snare of the fowler and from the deadly pestilence. He will cover you with His pinions, and under His wings you will find refuge; His faithfulness is a shield and buckler. You will not fear the terror of the night nor the arrow that flies by day, not the pestilence that stalks in darkness, not the destruction that wastes at noonday. A thousand may fall at Your side, ten thousand at Your right hand, but it will not come near you. You will only look with your eyes and see the recompense of the wicked. Because you have made the Lord your dwelling place—the Most High, who is my refuge no evil shall be allowed to befall you, no plaque come near your tent. For He will command His angels concerning you to guard you in all your ways. On their hands they will bear you up, lest you strike your food against a stone. You will tread on the lion and the adder; and young lion and the serpent you will trample underfoot. Because He holds fast to me in love, I will deliver him; I will protect him, because He knows my name. When He calls to me, I will answer Him; I will be with Him in trouble; I will rescue Him and honor Him. With long life I will satisfy Him and show Him my salvation* (Psalm 91:1-16).

When things are too much for me to bear, I fall into a deep meditation, asking God for guidance, and the silence helps me to hear God clearly. I did not have any strength to think negatively because I knew God did not bring me this far to leave me. While I was helping my children with their homework, I was praying; when I was cooking, I was praying. After putting my children to bed one evening, I took a long relaxing bath. I closed my eyes and prayed for peace of mind, a peaceful night's rest, and I asked God to speak to me.

I awoke to a beautiful morning, feeling well rested. After the morning rush of taking my children to school and heading to school myself, I spoke with my financial aid counselor. I told her what was going on, and she said she could not help me. She stated the only options I had were to pay by cash, take out a personal loan, or take a break from school for a while and work until I could pay for my tuition. I did not want to take any of those choices.

My heart was racing and I felt like I was going to have a nervous breakdown or a heart attack. I humbly walked out of her office and headed outside to catch my breath.

Cast all your anxiety on Him because He cares for you (1 Peter 5:7).

It was one major thing after another. At that moment, all I could do was cry and ask God why I was going through so much hurt and agony. What had I done to deserve this? I could not take it anymore. Then I remembered a paraphrase of a verse in Isaiah.

I will not cause pain without allowing something new to be born (Isaiah 66:9).

I began to breathe slowly, and as I did so I prayed for comfort and peace. Sadly, my counselor reassured me that there was nothing she could do. She said, "Again, Charlena, you can either take out a personal loan, work to pay off your schooling, or drop out of school. Those are your only options."

As I stood up, I looked her directly in her eyes, and said, "No, those are not my only options. I will find a way to finish and graduate."

She looked at me and said, "Okay, well good luck with everything." Sitting in my car in the school parking lot, so many thoughts were running through my mind. My rejection letter for aid was soaked by my tears as I pleaded to God for clarity and understanding.

But seek first the kingdom of God and His righteousness, and all these things will be added to you. Therefore do not be anxious about tomorrow, for tomorrow will not be anxious for itself. Sufficient for the day is its own trouble (Matthew 6: 33-34).

On my way to pick my children up from school, I had to get myself together because I could not let them see me worried or stressed. Later that night, after I put the kids to bed, I wrote in my journal, which always gave me a sense of peace. They were letters to God and helped me to become closer to Him. Going back and reading my journals always gives me hope to see that trouble does not last always. I asked God for help and guidance because dropping out of college was not an option for me.

I laid my head on the table and I awoke there in the morning. As I looked at a page in my journal, I remembered writing a month ago, "No cross no crown, everything worthwhile having is earned and it is not given." I wrote the statement down, meditated on it the entire day, and it gave me strength to make my next move.

The next day, I decided to apply to another college. I updated my financial aid forms so I could receive financial aid and use my refund check to pay for my college tuition at the school I was previously attending.

I asked God for insight and strength because I did not know how I was going to attend two universities fulltime, work, and take care of my children. I knew it had to be done somehow and in some way.

Someone might think this was not humanly possible, but I could not follow the path that was paved by other people. I had to step out in faith and follow God's lead.

When I was younger, my siblings and I used to take the short cut to the corner store. Grass did not exist there because the path was engraved with dirt. When I applied to the current school, I knew the grass was going to be tall, narrow, and I did not have a clue what was ahead of me.

That was the least of my worries because I knew God would not lead me in the wrong direction.

Your word is a lamp to my feet and a light to my path (Psalm 119:105).

I had to trust in God, and follow the path He designed for me.

By God's grace, I was accepted into the new university; however, the credits from the previous school I was attending would not transfer over. Although I had to start over, I did not look at it as a setback; I looked at it as a gift.

God was giving me the opportunity to continue to keep my grades up in order to continue to pay for classes at the previous school I was attending. The current school I was attending was on the semester system, which consist of sixteen weeks; the previous school was on the quarter system, and it consists of eleven weeks, which worked out perfectly.

I had enough money to pay for my classes at both schools! God was with me every step of the way. It was not easy, but God gave me the strength to execute all of my responsibilities and classes.

Mondays and Wednesdays I was taking four classes fulltime at the current university. On Tuesdays and Thursdays I was taking three classes full-time at the previous university I was attending.

Mondays through Fridays I was working after my classes; however, I always left work in enough time to pick my children up from the after school program and/or daycare. I would help them with their homework, cook dinner, talk about our day at the dinner table, spend time with them, and get them ready for bed.

Many days I pulled all-nighters because I had so many classes to study for and I could not get behind. For an entire year, I managed attending two schools at once, taking seven classes total, working, and taking care of my children.

When the Spirit of truth comes, He will guide you into all the truth, for He will not speak on His own authority, but whatever He hears He will speak, and He declares to you the things that are to come (John 16:13).

Believe it or not, with everything I had going on, I had a balanced schedule.

When I was attending the second school, it was completely different than the first one. When I was taking chemistry, we did not have any chairs in the lab. The professor said a chemist does not have time to sit down because we need to be alert at all times.

During statistics I was clueless because the professor went through each chapter as if he were the Road Runner. I had to put in more time and study extra hard for his class. When I took Ecology I could not believe I had to catch grasshoppers, mark them, send them back to the woods, and the next lab session I had to go back out to find the marked grasshoppers. I had to measure pine trees in the hot, scorching sun.

Needless to say, I was miserable. Those were the sacrifices I had to make to graduate from my current university. I was exhausted daily, but I did not have time to complain. It had to be done.

When I paid for my classes at the previous university I was attending, my financial aid counselor was surprised to see me. She asked me how I was paying for school because she looked in the system and saw that I had not taken out a personal loan. I smiled humbly and with grace. I kindly told her I prayed and trusted God, and He turned what I thought was impossible to the possible.

Do not be conformed to this world, but be transformed by the renewal of your mind, that by testing you may discern what is the will of God, what is good and acceptable and perfect (Roman 12:2).

When God steps into an impossible situation, it will always be a win-win situation. He is the only one who can turn anything around for the better. With that being said, I am blessed to know God.

Do not let negativity control your thoughts and turn your spirit into a depressing state to make you think it cannot be done. Turn the negative into a positive. Allow God to build a firm foundation around the thoughts of what's impossible to help you see that, with God, what's impossible can be possible.

The first step to the possible starts with believing and maintaining your faith in God. Ask God to give you inner and outer peace, peace of mind, peace in your home, and peace in your surroundings. Once peace is obtained, you can think and hear clearly from God. He will give you strength to believe in yourself and make the best out of the impossible.

Most of the time we are our own worse critic. We need to have a sharp mind, keen insight, and believe we are capable of anything that mentally and physically challenges us.

The beginning of wisdom is this: Get wisdom, and whatever you get, get insight (Proverbs 4:7).

Our mission is to change our situation for the better. We need to ignore and distance ourselves from people who continue to send negative energy our way.

We have to be optimistic and see the vision God wants to give us. We must have the courage to understand that we might face numerous failures, but trusting God and having patience, perseverance, and hope will turn any obstruction into harmony and joy. Each battle we face has a purpose; however, we must continue to ask for strength to endure it until the end.

Once we reach the end, we will find out why the battle took place. Most of the time, it answered questions that we asked for so long. As time goes on, we will have a sense of release and a peace of mind because everything happens for a reason. We will think differently and create a thicker layer of skin; after the storm, we will not be the same person as before.

I was lonely at the second university, and some of my classes were challenging. Although I did not know anyone on campus, I learned I could not be self-centered because I was never alone. Even when you think you are alone, you are not, because God is with you.

So do not fear, for I am with you; do not be dismayed, for I am your God. I will strengthen you and help you; I will uphold you with my righteous right hand (Isaiah 41:10).

Seeking success builds character. Everyone has the opportunity to gain insight from the impossible because dedication will turn it to the possible.

Make it a quest to never give up even when the dots seem as if they are difficult to connect. Keep a keen mindset, charge the battery of your mind, and know there is nothing impossible for God.

What, then, shall we say in response to these things? If God is for us, who can be against us? (Romans 8:31).

He will help us connect the dots so that we can see the bigger picture. Once we see the picture unfold, we need to be patient. We must be ready to prepare, respond, and execute when God tells us it is the right time. We should not move too fast because our short-term goals will determine our long-term commitments.

We shouldn't be ordinary; we should challenge ourselves and not just think inside the box. We should dare to be different and get out of the box. People who think inside the box are sometimes the ones who give the impossible its power. They are the ones who will take cover when they think the challenge is impossible. Instead of facing it head on, they will pull the lid of the box over their head out of fear.

They do not know the real meaning of the possible. Someone who is already out of the box and is not afraid to put on the armor of the Lord and stand up with courage to face anything that comes their way can face anything in God's strength.

And without faith it is impossible to please Him for whoever would draw near to God must believe that He exists and that He rewards those who seek Him (Hebrews 11:6).

God said we should only fear Him. We should not fear what man can do to us, nor should we fear troubled situations. Instead we need to stay prayed up, continue to have faith, and stay hopeful. We need to be different. Do not just think outside the box; get out of the box and face life and its challenges head on. Stand firm, hold fast, and know that God can turn the impossible to the possible.

Dear Father of all possibilities,

It is an honor to know what is impossible with man is possible for You. Life has a way of surprising us with unexpected news that seems unbearable, Lord. Thank You for blessing us with keen insight to know when to be still. There are so many distractions in the world today that try to sidetrack and shake our faith. Lord, keep our mind focused and steady on You. Amen.

❧ 9 ❧

ONE STEP CLOSER

Be on your guard; stand firm in the faith; be courageous; be strong (1 Corinthians 16:13).

Have you ever felt that you were at a standstill and sinking, that you were not moving anywhere fast, but going down, down, down? No matter what you do, nothing much ever goes your way; however, you continue to keep a positive attitude, walk with your head held high, and your shoulders broad with pride.

Numerous times I have felt I was in sinking sand and the more I gave my all, the more I felt exhausted, confused, tired, and impatient. I wondered about God's plan for me and how I should go about it. The harder I worked, the harder my mission became. I felt as if I were slowly but surely sinking further and further. Although I continued to pray for God's mercy and grace to prevent me from sinking, I often found myself sinking faster. I asked God what He wanted me to do and pled with Him to use me according to His will. Needless to say, I felt like I was being ignored because I never received an answer.

I applied for an emergency loan in graduate school. After attending a dentist appointment, I learned I needed three root canals. I did not have the funds to pay for them out of pocket; therefore, I applied for an emergency loan from school. One of the counselors from the financial aid department called me to address a situation about the aid I had received. I was told I owed the school more than nine thousand dollars because they had made a mistake and given me too much money.

I was highly upset because as a student I had trusted they knew how to perform their job correctly. I didn't deserve to be punished for their mistakes. I was not going to roll over and not put up a fight. I asked for a meeting with the head of financial aid, my financial aid counselor, my advisor in graduate studies, the dean of graduate studies, and the head of Student Academic Affairs.

I was surprised how fast I was granted the meeting. I felt as though I were one step closer to resolving the issue. Everyone showed up including my mother except for the dean of Graduate Studies who made up an excuse at the last minute why she could not make it. I was not surprised because every time things became heated in the Graduate department, the dean would either blame someone else, have someone else step in for her, or make up an excuse why she could not attend the meeting. Sadly, the dean never could sit in the hot seat because she always let someone else handle her responsibilities while she would step back and watch from a distance.

I enjoyed my journey in graduate school; however, after I realized the dean did not care about what was in the best interests for the students or her faculty and staff on numerous occasions, I was ready to complete the program.

During the meeting my advisor and I provided concrete evidence of why I should not have been accountable for the balance. However, the financial aid department did not want to own up to their mistakes. Instead, they wanted to pin it all on me. The head of Student Academic Affairs asked me in a nasty tone, "Charlena, why are we here and what do you want us to do?"

I replied, "I want my balance to be zero because I am graduating this quarter and you are telling me if I have a balance I will not be able to receive my degree, which I earned, or my transcripts. If I do not receive my transcripts, I will not be able to find work."

He replied in a nasty tone. "Correct. You have to pay off your balance before you can get your degree, and you cannot request your transcripts unless half of the balance is paid." He paused, rolled his eyes, and said in a harsh tone, "All you have to do is take out a personal loan and pay off the balance." I tried explaining to him that is easier said than done; however he cut me off and said, "I have better things to do, is the meeting over?" Clearly, my situation was not important, and it was crystal clear he did not care.

I stood up as he stood up and told him in a confident voice, "I am going to fight this because this is not fair to me as the student. I should not be punished for someone else's mistakes."

Stand firm let nothing move you (1 Corinthians 15:58).

He looked at me as he rolled his eyes, curled his lips tightly, and said, "Good luck."

I smiled at him with anger in my heart because I knew right then and there I had to put on the armor of God. I was not going to take this lightly.

Personally, I am not too fond of the word "luck"; I hope for a blessing. Before I left the room, I looked at everyone and I took up my cross and asked God to give me strength for each step I took.

Put on the full armor of God, so that you will be able stand firm against the schemes of the devil (Ephesians 6:11).

Right away, I called several lawyers to represent me, and God blessed me with one who was willing to represent me pro bono. Although I was grateful, after a year went by, he told me that I would have to settle the case and work out an agreement with the university or take them to small claims court myself. He reassured me that he would help me, but he said he thought we should settle. I told him, "Thank you, but no thanks." I refused to settle, thinking they could not get away with this.

A friend of mine suggested that I use her lawyer. I reached out to her lawyer and worked with her for a couple months. However, she continued to ask for more and more money. I refused to give her more money because I did not see any progress. Months later, I respectfully had to tell her I could not work with her anymore because she was representing my case for all of the wrong reasons—it was not to benefit me; it was to benefit her pockets and her reputation.

I began my search again, and I found a lawyer who was willing to take on the university; however, she charged a pretty penny for the consultation. After I paid, she started on the case right away; however, I found myself doing most of the work. She would ask me to conduct research that she should have done; after all, I was paying her to do the work.

After a year went by, she and the university lawyer were going back and forth. I thought I was one step closer to seeing some well needed results from this long journey. Sadly, the case wasn't moving forward; instead both lawyers were recycling papers that were already given to them from me and the school. I believe they continued this process to stall for time and to put more money in both of their pockets. Unfortunately I had to let her go too because I did not have more money and most importantly, no time to waste.

I kept thinking to myself, *I am supposed to be one step closer; instead I am thousands of steps behind.* I wasted time and money when I did not have either to spare. The only thing I could think to say is, "I can do all things through Christ who strengthens me" (Philippians 4:13). I fell on my knees to pray and asked God to direct my path, for I did know which road to take.

I was tired and exhausted from the years that had gone by without seeing any results. The quick sand became thicker, I could not move, and my body became paralyzed.

> *So then, dear brothers and sisters, be firm. Do not be moved!*
> *Always be outstanding in the work of the Lord, knowing that*
> *your labor is not in vain in the Lord* (1 Corinthians 15:58).

Once again I called on the Lord, and I heard God say, "Fear not, I've got you. This is a trial I prepared for you, and you do not need a lawyer, because I Am your lawyer. I Am going to use you, so people will know and see I Am real, I have all the power in My hands. I move mountains and I will make them crumble in the sea if I see fit."

I heard Him say, "Let me use you, why do you fear man when I made man lower than an angel" (Hebrews 2:7). "I Am is here. This is a trail I appointed for you because you are the chosen one to be used. There are going to be people who will say no, but you have to know I Am here and that is a part of My plan for you. Get ready to run this race because I will give you more endurance that you could ever imagine."

My brothers and sisters, consider it nothing but joy when you fall into all sorts of trials, because you will know that the testing of your faith produces endurance. And let endurance have its perfect effect, so that you will be perfect and complete, not deficient in anything (James 1:2-4).

It seemed like God said, "My grace and mercy is sufficient unto you and will not faint, grow weary or be tired. I Am your strength."

After I received and heard God's message, I humbly surrendered myself to Him. I did not have any doubts, and I immediately took up the cross I had laid to rest and faithfully threw it over my shoulders and said, "Lord, let's go, because I am ready!"

I sent out an emergency email to the students at the university to see if anyone was going through the same situation. I was surprised how many students were going through the same exact thing; however, only one other student was willing to take a stand. I called the local news and they filmed and broadcast the issue at hand.

The university started to wake up and realize I was not playing around. I wanted justice to be served. The one student who was willing to help took a step back after the news broadcast the film. For a quick second, I felt as though I were standing alone because I knew of so many of my fellow students who were going through the same thing as I was, however, they feared the consequences that could occur.

God made me aware this would happen in the speech He gave me, so I did not have any fear. I will admit I was disappointed because I could not believe how some people were willing to let the university rob them of their dignity and integrity.

Surely the righteous will never be shaken; they will be remembered forever (Psalm 112:6).

I felt the pressure, but I knew I was not alone. I gathered some facts and sent them to the university accreditation department; however, they replied my facts were not good enough. I sent the same documents to the radio station, the government, and to different law firms, but I did not get a response from anyone. God made me aware and prepared me for this obstacle too, and I said, "This too shall pass." I had so much endurance I was jumping over each hurdle without slowing down.

As time continued to pass, although I had some family and friends who doubted me, I also had several who were by my side, who prayed with me and encouraged me to keep moving forward.

I was very frustrated; I begin to think I was on a treadmill running, tired, and gasping for air. I refused to think I was not moving and only at a standstill. Quickly I started to fast and pray for clarity because I knew I could not throw in the towel.

Submit yourself, then to God. Resist the devil, and he will flee from you. Come near to God and He will come near to you (James 4:7-8).

Three years passed, I completed my masters in Healthcare Administration and started working on my PhD, worked as a professor, and I was still working hard on the case. I clearly remember one day when I was in my living room and prayed with a white candle burning until it went out. I sat for a while and meditated and asked God to give me insight on the next move to make.

I opened my laptop, looked up the university directory, and sent the director of the financial aid department an email. I expressed my thoughts as a former and dedicated student in their undergraduate and graduate program. She was the same person who told me when I was an undergraduate that I should change my major since I was not doing too well in my classes. I thought she was bitter because I proved her wrong when I walked across the stage with a degree I earned in Biology. I had faith in God because nobody knew what I was going through but our mighty Father. I waited patiently for her to email me back.

While I was waiting and praying, I made a cup of peppermint tea with a touch of lemon. I said, "Lord, while I am waiting, I know you are in the mix working something out." I did not have any fear in my spirit, nor did I have any worries. I only had faith in God because I knew He was working something out. I knew after three years I was one step closer to getting some results from this long journey, not to mention the fact that God knew my cross was rugged, and it was getting heavier and heavier.

I did not know if I had to carry it a little while longer, but if so, I knew God was going to give me the strength I needed to do so. I sat and looked at my email waiting for it to say I had an email in my inbox. She emailed me back right away.

She stated she talked to everyone who was in the meeting and they came up with an agreement, and we compromised to resolve this long lasting problem. I remembered reading Exodus 14:13-14,

> *Moses said to the people, "Do not fear! Stand firm and see the salvation of the Lord that He will provide for you today; for the*

*Egyptians that you see today you will never ever see again. The
Lord will fight for you, and you can be still."*

I did not realize how fast news spreads. After everything
was settled, my inbox was filled on a daily basis with students
who wanted me to assist them with the same situation. As I
read over the emails, most of them were from students who I
reached out to receive help from but who had been afraid to
come forward.

After three long years of working hard, in despair, full of
frustration, with a lot of heartache and pain, I declined to
help them. It was not because they did not help me, but I declined because they needed to grow and create thick skin, just
as I had.

Most importantly, this was a trial of my faith, and it
helped me become closer to God. If they followed through
with the case, the trial they would face would help them to
not only gain a layer of thick skin, but gain faith and bond
with God as well.

The three years before my breakthrough seemed as
though they had gone on forever, but God was preparing me
for more difficult challenges to come. Through this trial,
every single time when I thought I was one step closer to
completing my journey, one step turned into two steps, two
steps turned into a mile, and one mile turned into continuous
miles on my journey.

I realized I had to stop chasing after something I could
not do alone. I noticed when I was running on the treadmill
the scenery was still the same, but after I gave it to God the
scenery changed.

When we come to a dead end, we should seek and ask

God what is His will. When we get our answer, the question is, are we willing to complete the task that is laid out before us? When God guides our steps, more than likely our journey will have its up and downs, and we will have challenges and difficult times. There will be times when we will feel like giving up, but before we do that we should ask God for help, strength, peace of mind, courage, determination, and for His will to be done.

When we seek God's help, we will be one step closer to the finish line. Keep in mind there are going to be plenty of times when we can see the finish line, but sometimes God will take us on a detour. He knows we have more to learn, more to give, more to conquer, and He will give us the endurance we need to carry our cross on our detour.

Do not hesitate to follow His lead, for He knows what is best for us, and He knows how much we can bear. You will come out as a new and improved person. I know I did. I could hardly recognize myself, let alone other people.

I went into each situation fragile, but I always came out new, improved, stronger, wiser, and with impurity washed completely away. When we let God use us, it will be challenging, and it will not be an easy task. I learned throughout my trials that He was with me every step of the way, one step at a time, and with each step I was closer to earning my crown.

Most importantly, I came out knowing who God is, and I knew more than ever, with each step I was not only getting closer to solving my problem, but I was getting closer to God.

Dear Heavenly Father,

On this lovely day, the day that You have made, we will be glad and rejoice in it. With each stride it helps us to become a better person; and it will help us to create thicker skin. We will keep our mind focused on You. For You are the greatest; and with Your guidance, we can go the distance, we can take that extra mile, and we will have confidence to take that extra step. Amen.

❧10❧

UNWELCOME VISITORS

Fixing our attention on Jesus, the Pioneer and Perfecter of the faith, who, in view of the joy set before Him, endured the cross, disregarding its shame, and has sat down at the right hand of the throne of God (Hebrews 12:2).

At times in our lives we will come across people who appear to be to on our side. They are an expert at putting a smile on our face; furthermore, they are also veterans at giving us words of encouragement, but they do not have our best interests at heart. Secretly, they are filled with envy, waiting to hear and know our next move.

Do not be fooled. Sometimes these people can be a close family member, a childhood friend, or even our best friend. We have to realize we outgrow certain people; we mature and begin to think differently. Our minds are not as they were once before. The road that we traveled together has now divided and we are separated.

I had a friend once with whom I was talking one minute and distant the next. Over the years, my sister often told me she felt as though the friend was jealous of me, but I never took the time to notice. During our friendship, I used to tell her what I was doing and how I was going to go about executing my plan. I would talk to her about starting my own business, and she would say she wanted to do that too. I told her I was going to write a book, and she would say she was going to write a book too. Every time I wanted to do something, she wanted to do it too.

When things did not go as planned, I felt in my spirit that secretly she was happy I did not succeed. Never in a million years did I think she was against me instead of for me. Nearly every time I called her for support, she was also in a relationship and nowhere to be found.

We once got into a heated argument and she said, "'Everybody acts as if you are God; they always come to you for advice as if they cannot live their life without your approval.'" I was surprised she said that, but I knew right then and there after all these years I had welcomed an unwelcome visitor in my life.

I was trying to explain to her that there is no way I could ever compare myself to God. People talk to me because they feel comfortable with me and God sends them my way. I try to be honest and tell them the truth in regards to their situation.

She deeply expressed herself with, "No, they kiss your butt, and I am not going to kiss your butt." I told her nobody tries to do that, and I would not tolerate it if they did; however, people do value my advice and honesty. After she collected all her thoughts and spat them out like venom, I was shocked she felt that way about me. Her true colors came out after all the years we had known each other.

Am I now trying to win the approval of human beings, or of God? Or am I trying to please people? If I were still trying to please people, I would not be a servant of Christ (Galatians 1:10)."

Sadly, before she attacked me with her words, I had called to apologize for whatever I did or said wrong. I was the one who was always apologizing for what went wrong in our relationship. No, I am not perfect, I have my faults too, but I valued our sisterhood. She never apologized, and I never looked at our friendship the same after that conversation.

I tried continuing our friendship, but it wasn't savable. When the next guy came into her life, like always, she wasn't reachable, and I was fine with leaving well enough alone. Until this day I am deeply hurt because I treasured our sisterhood, but I constantly tell myself that sometimes people have different views on life.

Have you ever met someone and instantly you knew that person was an unwelcome visitor, but you went against your first instinct? We all invite unwelcome visitors into our lives, but we need to look at the signs head on, or we may get hurt.

An associate of mine and I were friends since middle school. I considered her to be one of my best friends. We both had our flaws as we all do, but I never understood her motives. At times she had the worst attitude, but I dealt with it because I thought maybe that was her character as a person.

We had our ups, downs, and fall outs, but we always talked things out and became friends again. When I had my son she was there for support both during and after the pregnancy. When I had my daughter she was there too. Sometimes I wondered where our friendship went wrong. There were a couple issues that made me second guess our friendship, such as she always wanted children. I felt she was jealous because I had children and she didn't. Her attitude would switch on and off like day and night.

I knew she needed my support as well, and I wasn't always there. When she pledged she said during her roughest times I wasn't there for support. I understood where she was coming from, but I couldn't always be there because I had children, but that wasn't an excuse. I should have been there.

When she had bought a house and had a house warming party, I didn't attend. It wasn't on purpose, but I made the choice not to deal with her attitude. Again, that wasn't a good enough excuse because I should have been there.

I believe as we got older, the seasons changed. When we were young adults, we were like two peas in a pod; but as we became adults, our seasons were shifting into different directions.

She thought I had the best of both worlds because I was in college and had children and she didn't. I thought she had the best of both worlds too because she was in college and she had freedom. I believe we both envied each other because we both had what the other person wanted.

We had a huge fall out. Years went by and a lot of time passed. One day, I reached out to her to say hello and to see how she was doing. She was living in New York and we made plans for me to visit for a week.

A couple months later I flew up to New York. She met me at the airport. I wanted to give her a hug when I saw her, but I noticed her attitude hadn't changed much. Instead we just greeted each other and started to walk to her apartment, which was three miles away. In my mind I was saying to myself, *You got to be kidding me.* I was strolling my luggage, had a book bag on my back, and another bag in my hand, not to mention it was around one hundred degrees in the middle of summer.

We walked in silence until we arrived at her apartment. Later that evening, we got something to eat, went to the market, and it was pleasant. I was stunned to see the apartments as they were the same as I saw on television. Later, we caught the train to her job—she worked at a library in Manhattan.

The following morning, I heard her get up; I got up as well to get ready. After a while I noticed she was gone. I waited because I thought maybe she went to the store. Time was ticking, and before I knew it thirty minutes passed by. I called her to see where she was, and she said she was headed to work. I was angry because she had not said she was going to work. She saw me getting ready and left the house without even saying good bye.

I packed my things because I was not going to deal with her nasty attitude as I did in the past. Her brother asked me to stay and go to work with him. I declined. I went with my first instinct, waved for a cab, and ask him to take me to Kennedy Airport.

I arrived at the airport, not knowing where to go. I asked the attendant for a ticket back to Georgia, however, the ticket was around six hundred dollars. I thought that was crazy since I had paid only around three hundred dollars for a round trip ticket to New York.

I had two options—either pay for the round trip ticket or stay a week in New York alone. I made the decision to stay in New York. The attendant was nice enough to help me find a hotel near the airport. I called my mother and she put money in my account to help with the hotel stay and for food. I made the best of my time in the Big Apple alone.

Later that day, my associate called, apologized, and asked

me to come back because she made plans for us. I decline her offer because I refused to be treated unkindly. I saw that she hadn't changed one bit. I asked God to lead the way and protect me in a city that I did not have a clue about.

The next morning I was on a mission. After I ate breakfast at the hotel since it was complementary, I made it out in enough time to board the tour bus. The guy asked me where I was from and my name. He was taken back when I said I was from Atlanta, Georgia. He addressed me as "Hotlanta." I thought that was funny. It was God and me hanging together all day and it was amazing!

We rode by the largest and oldest cemetery in New York. We visited the Statue of Liberty, which was a site to see. In order to get to the Status of Liberty we had to take a boat, and the background of New York and New Jersey were breathtaking! I did not get off the boat because I did not want to get on the New Jersey boat by mistake.

Afterwards, we visited the Empire State Building. It was a long line to reach the top, then there were many elevators to get on to reach the top. When I finally made it to the top of the Empire State Building, it was incredible! I had a stranger take a picture of me overlooking the skyscrapers.

Later we visited the memorial of the Twin Towers where they were building waterfalls. Although I did not personally know anyone who died in the 911 explosion, it was still very emotional. Towards the ending of our trip we rode by the library where they filmed *Ghostbusters*, and then they took us to Fifth Avenue, the Rockefeller Center, and NBC Building. My second day in New York was exciting to say the least!

The very next day, I decided to take a taxi cab to Times Square. It was a long, expensive ride. It started to rain and I had on flip flops. Go figure. I had to buy an umbrella and some tennis shoes, which weren't in my budget.

What began as a bad experience turned out to be amazing! The bright lights were unbelievable. I always wanted to taste New York pizza, and it turned out to be the best pizza I ever had in my life. I walked around Times Square for about two hours, enjoying the beautiful scenery.

I did not know it was a challenge to call a taxi cab. As I had seen done on television I held my hand out, but everybody would take my cab. I monitored other people to see how in the world they were pulling taxi cabs. They were good at it and made it look easy, but it wasn't.

After about ten people took my taxi cabs, I decided to step out in the street, yelled to the top of my lungs, and wave my hand in the pouring rain. Finally, a driver stopped for me. Goodness, I did not know it was that difficult to get a taxi cab in New York.

The fourth day I stayed in my hotel. I only took the shuttle bus to the airport to get my dinner and headed back. Day five, I was heading back to Atlanta.

After my experience in New York, I learned that it is okay to let bygone be bygones. We have to learn how to leave well enough along. I had thought I was mending a relationship and that I owed it to her to at least try.

Owe no man anything, but to love one another (Romans 13:6-7).

I felt as though I were an unwelcome visitor, by the way I was treated. However, God turned the unexpected experience into an abundance of experiences that were full of peace, happiness, and joy.

Unwelcome visitors are what I call battling distractions.

They will weigh us down with their negativity and secret jealousy, but we must be strong enough to break their chains. God does not intend for us to carry an unnecessary load when it is not the cross He has for us to bear.

Have you noticed that unwelcome visitors always have much to say about you and your life? They are negative, self-centered, and spiritually bankrupt. When the negative energy of unwelcome visitors compels us, we have to know when to express our thoughts in a correct way. We have to pray that they will find peace.

I believe unwelcome visitors are not well within themselves. They would rather live their life through someone else, or they would rather dwell in self-pity alone. They react differently around others.

Sometimes we focus on not expressing our thoughts because we do not want to hurt the feelings of the one we love, but God does not intend for us to carry someone else's cross. If indeed we love that person, we should not be afraid to speak the truth. Confronting someone's actions is progress toward increasing our peace of mind. After we respectfully voice our opinion, we need to let it go and move on.

Unwelcome visitors may put us in a position where we will forget who we are as a person and lose ourselves. Their bad habits become our habits without us even knowing. We shouldn't ever give anyone power over us to the point where we do not know who we are anymore. Transformation can come in a negative matter, and only we can prevent that.

Do not be conformed to this world, but be transformed by the renewal of your mind, that by testing you may discern what is the will of God, what is good and acceptable and perfect (Romans 12:2).

Some people think the grass is greener on the other side because other people make it appear that way, just to distract you. I used to look at other people situations. As years went on, I realized one's grass cannot always be green if it doesn't have any showers and storms in life. In order for grass to grow and be green, it has to be watered often. If the sky is always sunny and bright, there is no way the grass will grow and become greener. It will become brittle, dry, and it will change colors and eventually die. Unless their grass is synthetic, most definitely you will see that people with green grass have been surprised with numerous battles.

When we think about it, people who seem to have trouble-free lives are often the same ones who are still in the same place after time has passed. Their synthetic grass is still shining green, but the one catch is that it hasn't grown because they haven't received showers and battled the storms of life.

We have to ask ourselves if engaging with them in a battle is something we want to attempt. If so, good luck, because we will be running on a treadmill, fatigued, drained, tired, and out of breath. We will be in the same place, running, but we will not be moving anywhere. We need to dismiss our unwelcome visitors; all we can do is pray for them and let God handle the rest.

I believe in spreading the Word! God's Word can turn non-believers into believers. In undergraduate school, I came across a young lady in my Public Speaking class. She was always depressed, unhappy, and appeared to want to disappear into the crowd. One day, we were assigned to work together on our debate presentation.

I always read *Our Daily Bread,* and I took a chance to give her a copy. She told me she did not believe in God, so I told her, "Whenever you are in quiet place, take time to read the booklet; after you read it, if it is not your cup of tea at least you can say that you gave it a shot."

I am saying this for your benefit, not to place restrictions on you. I want you to do whatever will help you serve the Lord best, with as few distractions as possible (1 Corinthians 7:35).

God works in ways we cannot ever imagine. This young lady, who was once in despair from battling negative energy, now wears clothing filled with bright colors! They were full of light, her energy was followed by grace, and her attitude displayed the definition of faith that wasn't there before. One day, we had lunch together, and she expressed to me how she felt alive and well. She had tears coming down her face as she said she felt free of the dark spirits and darkness as she walked toward the light. She was clearly battling the enemy and full of distractions. Until this day, she and I are good friends.

She joined a church and got baptized, she is involved in her church, and now she is in missionary school to become a preacher. What a mighty God we serve when we dismiss unwelcome visitors and turn over our battles of distractions to Him!

At times we can be our own unwelcome visitor, due to our negative thinking. The worse distractions we face are ourselves. Last but not least, we battle a serious side effect of how to increase our funds to pay our bills, take care of our family, and handle life's responsibilities.

Sadly, we are our worst critics and slowly but surely can drift away from God.

But all too quickly the message is crowded out by the worries of this life, the lure of wealth, and the desire for other things, so no fruit is produced (Mark 4:19).

We cannot let distractions take control over our life. They will hold us back, block our blessings, make us feel unwanted, depressed, worried, and limit our possibilities. God will take on our battles and He will cease our distraction. What are you battling in life and who or what are your distractions? Ask yourself if this person or thing is worth invading your personal space and peace of mind.

Do not let the constant reminder of what other people think of you or their envy of you crowd and clutter your mind. Free yourself from their deceiving and envious ways. Forward them to God—He will be more than happy to take over.

Father,

The world has its way of tackling and weighing us down by the battles of distractions. With humble hearts we pray for our unwelcome visitors. You have revealed to us over and over why some people should not be welcomed in our life. Lord, we need Your help with parting ways from our distractions. We ask, Lord, that You keep us paddling and moving upstream to find peace and joy. We now realize we have a chance of receiving happiness, peace, and the unconditional love You have chosen for us. Amen.

ॐ11ॐ

A SEASON FOR EVERYTHING

There is a time for everything, and a season for every activity under the heavens: a time to be born and a time to die, a time to plant and a time to uproot, a time to kill and a time to heal, a time to tear down and a time to build, a time to weep and a time to laugh, a time to mourn and a time to dance, a time to scatter stones and a time to gather them, a time to embrace and a time to refrain from embracing, a time to search and a time to give up, a time to keep and a time to throw away, a time to tear and a time to mend, a time to be silent and a time to speak, a time for war and a time for peace (Ecclesiastes 3:1-8).

As the season changes, so does our life. The scenery changes and it stimulates our mind to embrace the spring breeze, the summer bright colors, the fall crisp air, and the cozy winter chills.

God sees potential in us and He knows how much we can bear. He places hurdles in front of us that we can jump over if necessary to create endurance to finish our journey. We cannot let the devil make our weakness a perfect match for his destruction. The devil is trying to corrupt our mind to transfer to it doubt about God and about ourselves. We should not give him power to do that. We know that God has all the power and no harm can come to us.

And let us not grow weary of doing good, for in due season we will reap, if we do not give up (Galatians 6:9).

God can turn any situation around for the better, and the best thing of all is that we can call on Him in the morning, evening, midnight hour, when we are driving our car, when we are happy, when we experience stress, and when we feel like we have no strength left.

God is the only way to have peace in our mind, in our soul, and in our lives. We have to let go and let God take over our situations because the battle is not ours, it is the Lord's battle, and the battle is already won.

Life's struggles may have us second guessing ourselves. We might think from time to time that the battle is not already won because it seems as though it is never ending. I have good news for you! Life's struggles are the seasons of change.

While the earth remains, seedtime and harvest, cold and heat, summer and winter, day and night, shall not cease (Genesis 8:22).

When we look at the leaves on the trees during the summer season they are breathtaking because we admire their beauty and structure. However, do we think about the struggles and the process the tree had to go through for it to become so strong, hydrated, and healthy?

The summer is the tree's "daylight savings time," when the sun stays out a little longer and the trees have their chance to produce food. That is why the leaves on the trees are so vibrant.

As the seasons change, fall quietly steps in. Many of the leaves tend to change colors, turning to brown, orange, gold, red, and sometimes multicolored. As the season progresses we lose hours of daylight, therefore, the sun is not shining as much and the trees are not producing as much food as they need to stay hydrated and vibrant.

The leaves on the trees in the fall are gorgeous, and the wind complements the leaves as they float carefree in the air. The leaves gently land on the ground, leaving the branches bare as winter approaches. Although the branches are bare, they are not brittle; they are in the process of revival and renewing their strength.

Eventually the cold winter passes while the trees are in their relaxing state, and spring comes peeking in as bright as the sun. Days are longer and warmer as the hours of sunlight lengthen once again. As the season of spring breaks through, the leaves begin to use their renewed strength to sprout and unfurl. Their colorful flowers begin to add a touch of tenderness and softness as some of them bloom and some are waiting patiently until the time is right.

As the seasons change, the leaves change, but the trees still have a firm foundation with their roots deep beneath, giving them stability. The rooted stability allows the branches to be steadfast as the leaves come and go.

From the fig tree learn its lesson: as soon as its branch becomes tender and puts out its leaves, you know that summer is near (Matthew 24:32).

God is our deep root and stability as the seasons change in our lives. When our troubles take a toll on us, we are like the leaves when the seasons change during the summer, fall, winter, and spring. We change as we live freely; as our season changes, our trials and tribulations shake our boughs, renewing our strength.

As the challenges tempt us to give up, God changes the seasons so we can encounter a different viewpoint. As the scenery changes, our situation fades in the background, and almost without noticing it, the worries have departed.

God works within and through us as we release our stress and turn it over to Him. We have to realize we cannot worry and stress over the things we cannot change. It is easier said than done. I know for a fact that I do not have to worry about the things I cannot control because the battle is already won. We might not see it at the moment, but we must steadfastly keep the faith and believe it.

He is like a tree planted by streams of water that yields its fruit in its season, and its leaf does not wither. In all that he does, he prospers (Psalm 1:3).

We have to step back and trust that all will work out for the better and according to God's will. We are God's children and like children sometimes we can get in God's way. I remember when my children were babies, sometimes when I was cooking they tended to get in my way. I would either stumble over them or trip over myself because I didn't want to step on their tiny fingers or toes.

When it became too much, I would sit them in the living room and tell to stay there. Somehow they would find their way back into the kitchen, sitting near my leg or pulling up on my leg as they held on to my pants, or they would just sit there and be in my way.

Sometimes I would stop what I was doing and pick them up. I would play with them, put them in their high chair, or rock them in my arms until they fell asleep. That way, I would be able to cook without worrying about them being in the way and getting harmed.

History repeats itself because my grandmother had her seasons too just as I did.

> *He changes times and seasons; he removes kings and sets up kings; he gives wisdom to the wise and knowledge to those who have understanding* (Daniel 2:21).

I remember when my sisters and I were little girls we used to always be in the kitchen when my grandmother was cooking her one-of-a-kind cornbread, pound cakes, or good old-fashioned southern butter biscuits.

My grandmother's kitchen was smaller than the kitchen in my apartment. Regardless, it did not matter how small her kitchen was, my siblings and I played with the pots and pans, and she managed to move around without stumbling over us.

When she turned on the oven to bake the biscuits, cornbread, or cakes, she would tell us to leave the kitchen because she didn't want us to get burned. I must say, my grandmother was wiser in handling the situation because I'm sure my mother and her siblings used to be in the kitchen as well.

Sometimes we can be in God's way; however, He is so gentle with us that He never stumbles over us. He listens to us, but He sees in advance when what we are asking for would not be best for us. We must trust and believe God wants what is best for us. When we get an answer and the answer is no, I do believe He is sad when we cry. But as time goes on, He smiles because we gain a clearer understanding of His answer.

When we let God use us, it is challenging, and it is not always an easy task. However, He is with us every step of the way, one step at a time; and with each step, we are one step closer to earning our crown.

The seasons in our life change. Time can either make us

stronger and wiser or we can dwell in pity and sorrow; it is our decision. If we conquer the seasons, if we trust and believe God has everything worked out as the seasons change, we can feel at ease knowing we are protected. For we do not know what the future may hold, but we do know all things work together for our good.

It is not for you to know times or seasons that the Father has fixed by his own authority (Acts 1:7).

As I talked about earlier, change may be too simple and easy. It does not allow us to dwell on the situation as we take a shortcut to solve the issues at hand. Trust in God and know sometimes He would rather for you to go around the issues at hand instead.

When we go around, it gives us more comfort and peace. It gives us more time to focus on God, we can hear Him more clearly, and our eyes are keener because we can see clearer. Our emotions are not on a roller coaster shifting gears, and we have more time to endure the changes of the seasons when we are going around instead of going through them. It might take a lot longer going around the storm instead of enduring the gusty wind, showers, and cloudy skies all at one time by going through it.

When going around, a larger storm might occur, but we will be prepared and know the patterns of the weather because God is using us to become closer to Him. The sun will shine, or the sun will hide behind the clouds to give us shade. The flowers will be so amazingly beautiful, and we will be able to have more than enough time to admire their color, unique shapes, and smell.

By going around, the wind will be more like a summer breeze, giving us the ability to brace ourselves for the storms that lie ahead. We will have more time to relax in peace and let God use us as He see fit.

Give the long way around a chance—it will clear out the cobwebs and it will bring out balance in your life. Going around the storm with pure motivation will produce growth as you practice patience. Patience brings change, integrity, and perseverance. We will have a better understanding of the outcome of our past and present seasons, and also the seasons that are to come.

When the seasons change, we must have perseverance. Despite the difficult times, we should always have a mindset to speak and think positively during opposition because then we have a purpose for living. We will then know when our seasons are changing, and we are on the verge of achieving our harvest.

When we find ourselves in what seems to be an unchanging situation, we need to know that it will eventually change—it is just taking longer than expected. That is when we have to practice what God instructed us to do and that is to be at "Peace, be still." We need to learn how to utilize our time and prepare for our breakthrough. If we do not sow, we cannot reap; if we do not reap, we cannot produce.

The seed which fell among the thorns, these are the ones who have heard, as they go on their way they are choked with worries and riches and pleasures of this life, and bring no fruit to maturity. "But the seed in the good soil, these are the ones who have heard, and hold it fast, and bear fruit with perseverance" (Luke 8:14-15).

In life most things mature slowly, and in their right season they will sprout. For example, before a baby is born, the egg must be fertilized. The next step would be the egg would become a zygote. The early stage of development and cell division is called an embryo. During the process of the ninth week he/she is called a fetus. As the fetus develops, it is recognized as a baby. For nine months as the baby develops, he/she is protected by his/her mother as she waits patiently for precious time to pass as the seasons change for the arrival of her blessing.

> *Like newborn babies, long for the pure milk of the word, so that by it you may grow in respect to salvation* (1 Peter 2:2).

Spring is for planting the seed because the morning dew is perfect! It has the right amount of sun and the breeze is blowing gently to mold the seed in its rightful order.

Summer is for growth because the sun rises at the right time and sets later in the evening to feed the developing seeds as we wait patiently.

Fall is for the harvest, as we gather and collect it. During the harvest we have to make a decision to either keep unwelcome visitors in our life or move forward with producing peace in our life. Our harvest season is to enable us to produce action.

Winter is for recovery as we rest and take it easy to see what our hard work will produce in our upcoming seasons.

In order to reap from the planting of the seeds, it takes time and patience. We have sowed and produce our harvest. It is hard and time consuming, but we cannot give up.

Keep in mind the most important time is the time of the planting. Planting involves our faith and frame of thinking. What we plant in, our mind shall be. If we continue to think negatively in our challenging seasons, we need to stop and re-examine our life and correct our mistakes.

Now he who supplies seed to the sower and bread for food will supply and multiply your seed for sowing and increase the harvest of your righteousness (2 Corinthians 9:10).

After we correct our mistakes, then we need to wait patiently as our seasons change for the better. We must face the challenges as the seasons change, and we must also own up to our mistakes. We must have the courage to want to change because change is an opportunity for planting and growing. As we change our ways of thinking and allow growth to produce our harvest, our greatest opportunity is a touch away from making a tremendous difference in our life.

Father of all seasons,

I know You know what is best for me, and if going around leads to a better understanding and the ability to become closer to You, I prefer to take the longer route if it is Your will. I know I will gain more insight, patience, and perseverance. My life can be so overwhelming; restore my peace in my inner being. Rejuvenate my life and soul; I am not worried about the seasons changing. I am leaving my worries at Your feet, for You are the One who can provide me with peace in my mind, heart, and soul. Lord. I give it all to You. Amen.

❧12❧

THE MEANING OF FORGIVENESS

Be kind and compassionate to one another, forgiving each other, just as in Christ, God forgave you (Ephesians 4:32).

We might look at forgiveness as a form of weakness, being caught up in a net with no way out, or as a desperate act of robbing ourselves by letting go of the suffering someone has caused us.

We might think we failed ourselves by forgiving the person who stabbed us in the back or of the backbiting, dishonesty, and suffering they inflicted on us. When we think of extending forgiveness, our heart may become colder than it was before. We think to ourselves that we do not want them to win or to think what they did to us is acceptable. They will win if we continue to hold on to unforgiveness, and we will lose ourselves as a person if we do not let go.

I used to think I was doing an unjustice to myself because I carried around a load of baggage from having a heavy heart. The baggage I carried weighed me down. I was stressed, unhappy, always in a defensive mode, and was distracted emotionally. I let the hurt and pain someone put on me strip my identity and corrupt my character. I did not smile because I was filled with so much anger. I gave them power over me. I gave them my freedom; and sadly, I gave them my life. I was drained because I let unforgiveness suck the life out of me.

It took some time for me to forgive. As a matter of fact, it took me two years to forgive my ex-husband, and it took me a year to forgive my siblings. I had a choice to either let the rain make me bitter or to forgive. God gave me the strength to forgive because I couldn't go on living in the dark. I realized as long as I am living, I am going to see the best and the worst in people. Most importantly, I came to realize I want to be happy and live a peaceful life. In order to do that, it is up to me how I go by letting things and what people do affect me.

He has granted us new life to rebuild the house of our God and repair the ruins (Ezra 9:9).

I was restored from the agony and suffering I endured. The torture from the scars was healed, and what was once a damaged, bruised heart had life once again. How? First, I made peace with myself because I knew I deserved to be happy. I earned the right to smile, laugh, cry tears of joy, and enjoy a beautiful day, listening to the rain fall as I relaxed with a calm, sound mind. I came to the conclusion that nobody had the power to take away what I've earned—a well deserved, wonderful, and peaceful life.

I also made peace with my ex-husband. I called him and said, "I forgive you." He said, "Forgive me for what? I did not do anything wrong."

I humbly said, "If you feel that way, and you are fine with your decision, that is okay with me, but I want to say, I forgive you and I will keep you in my prayers." I asked him if he could forgive me for my wrong of not being the wife he expected of me. He said that he forgave me. I said, "Thank you.

Is your mother at home? I would like to speak with her." He said his mother did not want to talk to me so instead, I wrote his mother a letter and expressed my thoughts in a respectful manner. I asked her for forgiveness and told her in the letter that I forgave her and would keep her in my prayers. I never heard back from his mother, and that was okay with me.

Finally, I was happy with my decisions. I felt a sense of relief. It had been a long time coming, but I knew how to genuinely smile again. I looked in the mirror and admired my smile. Before I knew it, I was laughing and praising God for giving me the strength to forgive, love, and live life once again. God restored my soul mentally, emotionally, physically, and spiritually.

I have suffered the loss of all things, and count them as rubbish, that I may gain Christ (Philippians 3:8).

After God blessed me with the strength I needed, it was easy for me to pray, repent, and ask for forgiveness in order to be rejuvenated within my heart. I had to start with myself first; and after I worked on myself, I asked God for clarity and strength to teach me the true meaning of forgiveness. Nevertheless, I did not know that what I was asking for was going to be such a challenge. I must say, what I asked for taught me the real meaning of forgiveness.

After picking my son up from school one day, I noticed he had a hoodie and phone that did not belong to him. Several times I told him to take both the hoodie and phone back to the people they belonged to, but he refused to listen. I told him to walk home from school so that he and I could cool down. Instead of walking home, he made the choice to call my niece, and my sister picked him up from school.

Although my sister and I weren't on good terms, she

called me and let me know what my son was saying about me. My son told so many lies on me, saying I hit him with a crutch, and that I treated him differently from my other children. I was hurt and disappointed. I kept wondering why would my son say terrible things about me. I live for my children and I will give my children my last.

The next day, when I picked my son up from school, I confronted him about the lies he had told about me, and he said he did not say any of the above. I put my sister on speaker phone while my son was in the car and he admitted he said those things about me. However, he also admitted he lied to receive a pity party on his behalf. That hurt me so badly.

I was torn between my emotions, and I needed a break for one night to think clearly. A friend let my children spend the night at her house, and I picked them up the next day. She called me later that day and said she believed my son stole her phone. I did not think twice about it because for some reason my son was desperate for a phone. He wanted to fit in with the in crowd. I had preached to my children that when they wanted something so badly that they would do anything to get it, it most definitely would not do them any good. I asked my son if he had her phone, and he said no. I knew he had her phone, so I agreed to pay for her phone and to pay to disconnect her service, which would cost almost nine hundred dollars. I did not have the money to do it; however, I wanted to do what was right.

One day, I remembered my son called me from a friend's phone several days before, and I had saved the number. God works in mysterious ways, I called the young man and I asked him if he knew my son had a phone. He replied yes, and he described the phone, and it was my friend's phone. I was beyond hurt combined with anger because my son knew I was going to have to pay off my friend's contract. However, he did not care; he wanted a phone so badly that he would do anything to keep it, even if I paid off her contract with my last dollar.

I thanked God for letting me get to the truth, and I asked my son again about it, and he lied again. I told him I knew he had the phone because his friend told me he did. My son had no choice but to admit the truth, and I was able to give my friend her phone back. I was so hurt because my own child was casting pain on me without a care over and over again.

Months later, I took my daughter to get a physical at an in-store clinic because she wanted to cheer for her school. I gave my son some money to buy me a chocolate bar. He bought the chocolate bar and brought it to me and I thanked him. Never in a million years had I thought someone was watching and listening. The nurse practitioner called my daughter back and I went in the room with her. I told my oldest son to watch his brother until my daughter and I came out from getting a physical. I never thought I was going to walk into a pit.

As my children and I were walking out of the store, a random guy, dressed with a fishing hat, shorts, and carrying around a shopping basket asked me if he could speak to me. I said no and kept going. He said, "Ma'am, I really have to speak to you." I knew right then and there he was an undercover police officer.

My children and I walked into the stock room of the store. He told me my oldest son opened up a bag of Reese's and was eating them, and he had my little one with him. I was crushed and my heart could not take any more bad news from my son's actions.

The officer asked my son why he ate the Reese's and he said, "Because my mom never pays me any attention." I looked at my son and words could not describe how I felt. My heart could not sink anymore. I was speechless, and I wanted to tell the officer to lock him up. I was sick of my son lying to me over and over again because he wanted to get himself out of his own mess once again. I could not believe my son would throw me in front of the bus again. This time it was not a family or friend, it was an officer of the law.

The officer told my son, "I failed to realize your mother did not pay you any attention because I do not hear mothers tell their child thank you." He had heard me thank him after he came back with my chocolate bar and receipt. That is why I said, you never know who is listening and watching you. The officer told my son, "The only reason why I am not going to lock you up is because of your mother. I see she has structure in the home; she loves and respects her children." The officer looked at me and he saw how hurt I was. He asked me, "Mom, what do you want to do, do you want me to lock him up and take him down to the station?"

I wanted to say, "Yes, so I can teach my son a valuable lesson since he said I do not pay him any attention." However, I had to think about myself since he was sixteen years old, I would have been responsible for his fees, maybe probation, taking him to do community service, and I was sure so much more. I did not have that time to spare because I had enough on my plate. I also thought about my son's wellbeing, including his reputation. I did not want to act out of hurt, selfishness, and exceeding pain. Instead, I told the officer if he did not mind, I wanted to take my son home because I did not want my son to have a record. He probably would not have gotten into college or obtained a decent job, and I know he would have been labeled for the rest of his life.

So many people have hurt me in my life and I have endured so much pain, but I never thought a child I carried, birthed into this world, and raised alone would throw me right in front of the bus over and over again. I told my son even a mother has enough and as he becomes older, if he keeps making decisions that are not right, I would not be able to save him.

I love my children, but I also have limitations. I never was so hurt in my life until my son cast pain on my heart. He set my heart on fire, and every time he would throw me in front of the bus, it was more gasoline cast on the fire he created.

My grandmother and father both told me actions speak louder than words. I started to second guess myself as to where I went wrong with my son. I was not the perfect mother, no one is, but I felt as though I raised him to the best of my being. I gave my children all and my last. I will give them my last breath if I had to, so I was hurt because not only was I raising my children alone, but my son had seen the hardship I have endured. My son's actions affected our relationship. I could not trust a word that came out of his mouth. I could not look him in the eye, I hardly talked to him because not only was I hurt from all of his encounters and lies, but I was highly upset.

As time went on I showed my son tough love. I showed him how it feels for a mother not to pay attention to their child. In caring for him, I only did what was required of me to do by law. I did not do anything more or anything less. As time went by, we grew further and further apart.

I asked God to show me the real meaning of forgiveness, and he used my son to open my eyes, heart, soul, mind, spirit, and truth to give me an example. God knew He could not use my ex-husband because he could not hurt me as much as my son did, nor was my ex-husband close to my heart and soul.

God did not use my family and friends because I could either let an offense fall off my back or continue to ignore them. The saying goes, "Out of sight out of mind." However, God used my son who is dear to me, whom I love with all my soul and heart. God gave me an answer to my question when I asked Him for clarity and strength to teach me the true meaning of forgiveness.

I did not know or understood the definition of forgiveness until it hit home, and it hit hard on my heart and within my inner being. I was torn between my emotions because I never thought my son would put his mother through the wringer.

It was hard for me to shake, and I prayed constantly because I was full of resentment. Every time I looked at my son, I resented him more and more, although he did not understand how much I was hurting. My heart and mind were set on "how can someone whom you carried, raised, and love so dearly say they love you, but constantly make you feel as if you are their enemy?" The scars were open and it was continuously painful.

During this battle of learning the true meaning of forgiveness and how to forgive, the bond I had with God grew closer and closer. As I fasted for a clearer understanding, I put my differences aside and spent more time with my son because I was concerned about why his actions were so brutal and selfish.

My son came to me one day, and said, "Mom, I miss the relationship we once had. We used to be so close." I reminded him that his actions spoke louder than his words. I missed the relationship my son and I had too, but I was tired of him constantly making me look like a bad mother.

Trust had been vanquished. I explained to him, regardless of how many times he tries to save himself, he will be accountable for his actions. I poured my heart out and expressed my thoughts with deep sympathy and affection. I listened to my son as well while he expressed his thoughts. I asked him what I had done wrong as a mother.

He cried with remorse and said, "Mom, you have done all you could do, and I am sorry. I am sorry, Mama." I felt in my heart he was sincere.

I opened my arms as he fell into them, I cradled my baby, and said, "I love you, and I forgive you. Please forgive me too." He looked at me and said, "Mom, you are the best mom that a son could ever hope for. Thank you for forgiving me. I miss you and the bond that we shared. I am going to be a better son and I am going to make better decisions."

A year has passed and I am a proud mother. He is now in the twelfth grade, going to high school and college at the same time, playing tennis, and working a part-time job. We are still working on trust, but each day is an improvement.

God is such as an amazing Father! When you ask Him for a clearer understanding, you better believe He will give you an answer.

As God has forgiven us many times for our sins, of course I forgave my son; however, it was a long journey in the making. The bruises healed slowly but surely, though I am still working on regaining trust in him.

Forgiveness is a powerful word that has a powerful meaning. It is also challenging because when you think you have forgiven someone, you may find it is not so easy to forget. I learned that we should not ever let someone burn out our fire.

If we have been hurt, we may tend to fall into a deep state of depression and stress, and be full of anger and resentment, which burns out our fire. The only way to keep the fire burning is to ask God to help us heal from such hurts and to teach us the real meaning of forgiveness.

The perfect gift we could give ourselves is the will to forgive. It will cleanse and heal our soul. It is not a loss of vengeance, it does not mean we lost—it is always a win-win situation. With each stride we take, we gain endurance and that is a form of bravery.

Forgiveness represents freedom, self-control, power, growth, and most importantly, it moves you to follow and create a bond with God. Forgiveness is the beginning of freedom.

Forgiver,

How can we not forgive when You have forgiven us numerous times? Thank You for helping us understand that forgiveness starts with us in our heart, mind, and soul. Forgiveness is the most challenging journey we have to conquer. As I walk in the Spirit, pray continuously, and be focused on You, You never led me astray. I know as You bless me to see another day, I will have a better and clearer understanding of the true meaning of forgiveness. Thank You for Your forgiveness and unconditional love. Amen.

❧13❧

SOURCE OF HOPE

Jesus said to his disciples, whoever wants to be my disciple must deny themselves and take up their cross and follow me (Matthew 16:24).

We all have a cross to bear; however, the question is, how will we carry our cross and the crosses yet to come? Will we seek God for guidance or look to our own understanding? If we look to our own understanding, we will always carry and bear the same cross without earning a crown. We will feel as though we are going around in a never-ending circle. Isn't our situation confusing enough?

We don't need a dizzy spell to make our situation more difficult than it should be. Sometimes we make things worse than what they are because we do not know how to ask God for help. We have too much pride, or we let what may seem to be the worst of things shake us up with fear.

When fear strikes, we lose hope and our faith shakes; we look to our own understanding and make tremendously careless mistakes. We become frustrated and want to throw in the towel.

I prayed to the Lord, and He answered me. He freed me from all my fears (Psalm 34:4).

We have to remember when push comes to shove and we

reach the bottom, soon we will find out we cannot make it alone. We need God's guidance, strength, and understanding. They are the only way to carry our cross and rightfully receive our crown. Keep in mind, each cross will be a challenge, some more challenging than others; but if we invite God on our journey, we will never ever be alone.

One day during the morning hours after being up all night with my son, listening to my husband worry about how we are going to pay our bills, and getting my oldest children together for school, I was beyond exhausted.

As I handed my little one over to my husband, I put my books in my book bag, ran around to pack the children's lunches, and made breakfast. My husband kept nagging me about all sorts of things that were not in my control. I asked him what he wanted me to do; he looked at me and continued to complain, whine, and nag.

I had a knife in my hand as I dipped it in the peanut butter jar. He continued to whine and started to cry. I was sick of it. I yelled, "What you want me to do?" As I yelled I moved my hand and cut the side of my wrist; when I looked down I only saw blood and the pink tissues sprouted out as if it were a cauliflower.

I couldn't afford to be in a state of shock because I had so much to do. I asked him if he could take the children to school while I drove myself to the emergency room. Before I left I put a sterilized non-stick bandage over the wound and wrapped my wrist with a bandage to prevent an infection.

After being admitted to the emergency room, I sat there and said to myself that there was no way I could continue on through this agony. The doctor came in the room with a long needle to stick in the tissue so he could numb and stitch up my wrist. He asked me what had happened. When I told him, he said, "Ma'am, this is none of my business, but I want to give you a word of advice. You were two inches away from your median nerve, and you could have bled to death. You need to let go and let God fight this battle."

I had to stay a little while because I was dehydrated. I wasn't surprised because I was moving here, there, doing this and that, and I wasn't taking care of myself. Honestly, I did not have time to think about myself because there was so much to do.

I was so tired; I slept through the throbbing pain. When I awoke I panicked because I knew time was not going to be on my side since I had so much to do. The physician came in and said, "Ma'am, I wanted you to sleep because I could not let you get behind the wheel exhausted and dehydrated. You needed some well needed rest."

When I left it was time for me to get the children from school. I felt rested, but I knew I was behind on my responsibilities, and the next day there was going to be triple work to do.

On my way to get my children, I had a long talk with God. I begged Him to lift the load off my shoulders. I felt like I was going to go insane if I continued to live that way. My wounds were open emotionally, mentally, and physically.

I prayed for peace in my surrounding, heart, mind, and soul. I knew sooner or later God was going to heal my wombs and scars.

He heals the brokenhearted and binds up their wounds (Psalm 147:3).

Later that evening after the children were asleep, my husband and I got into a heated argument. He laid on the floor with the Bible open, crying about him not having a job. This was a daily routine for him, and I did not understand his motive. I tried to be supportive, but it took a toll on me because all he did was hover over the Bible and act depressed.

He also followed me around the house, nagging and in a state of stress. I did not know what to do anymore. I did not know what he wanted from me. I wasn't a super woman and I did the best I could. However, the blame was always placed on me. I took a shower and found myself falling asleep in the shower because that was the only peace I had when I was around him.

This marriage changed me as a person and snatched the happiness out of my life. I became someone whom I didn't know. I cried silently at night, asking God, *Why me?* When I looked at myself in the mirror I couldn't recognize myself.

I looked at my hands—they were weak but yet strong because of the role I had to take on. My feet were worn and throbbing from pacing back and forth, caring for my little one, up all day from taking care of my family, going to school, and taking care of my home. I forgot how to enjoy life because I was always on the go.

I sacrificed so much for my marriage and for my family. Every day, I felt like I did not have anything left to give, but when I looked at my babies I knew I had a reason and a purpose to live, to keep working hard, and to give my all, because better days were ahead.

I felt my faith slipping, but I could not let it get away from me completely. I changed up my routine.

And be renewed in the spirit of your mind (Ephesians 4:23).

Before I went to class I would sit in my car to have "me" time. I would pray, meditate, and claim peace in my life and surroundings. Before going home I would take my children to the park, and I learned how to laugh and smile again. I would make a picnic basket and take it to the park and lie out on our blanket and look at up at the sky. It was a peace of serenity and hope.

Every day, I renewed my mind with the Word. I stepped out in faith daily, claiming today was going to be better than yesterday. Awaking to a new day, I smiled because I was breathing, living, in my right mind, and blessed. I cherished each day and walked with my head up, claiming peace and harmony with every step I took.

When my husband fell into his pity party, I would tell him all we can do is pray about it and do our part as well. I let that be and went on about my day. I smiled making dinner, cleaning the house, helping the children with their homework, etc. I smiled because I felt the love and peace of God surrounding me.

One day, I washed my face and found myself looking in the mirror. I smiled because I knew exactly whom I was looking at. I laughed and praised God because I was renewed and better than I was before.

Now the Lord of peace Himself give you peace always by every means. The Lord be with you all (2 Thessalonians 3:16).

We serve a mighty God and nothing is impossible for Him. Every time I visit the beach, I sit on the balcony or dig my feet in the sand as I look at the never-ending ocean. I observe the waves and listen to the them play a tune. I think it is amazing how during the morning and afternoon hours, the waves distance themselves from the shore. However, during the evening, the waves cover the shore entirely.

I think to myself how we serve an amazing God because the waves obey His command. There is no one who can tell me there is not a God because as I look at the ocean, nobody knows the depth of the sea, people only assume. We do know it obeys God's command by limiting its width of how wide it should spread and how long it should reach.

He got up, rebuked the wind and said to the waves, "Quiet! Be still!" Then the wind died down and it was completely calm. He said to his disciples, "Why are you so afraid? Do you still have no faith?" (Mark 4:39-40).

Isn't God incredible! Why wouldn't we want an incredible God to help us carry our cross? If we are faithful to Him, we will earn our crown because God knows we were a faithful servant, and it was well earned and deserved.

Life offers so many challenges, people, and situations that will throw us out to the wolves. We will often be in an odd environment, and we will have to fight for what we want. Though we may know people who would like to throw us to the wolves, if we have God on our side, we can believe and know we will come back leading the pack because His grace is sufficient.

That is what I call the big come back. Those who aimed to hurt us will realize we cannot be broken or tarnished, nor are we afraid to come back leading the pack. That takes courage, growth, and strength.

Our enemies and detractors fail to realize they made us a better person; they helped us earn a well-deserved crown. As time goes by, they are irrelevant as they fade in the background, standing in the same spot and doing the same thing. People like that rarely move forward because they only try to hurt or bring other people down to their level. They will never understand that they are helping other people to walk through the fire head on and come out strongly leading the pack.

God knows exactly how to make us a stronger person physically, emotionally, and mentally. Most of the time we do not have an understanding, but He does as He watches over us and proudly puts the crown on our head when we successfully and spiritually execute our journey.

Carrying our cross helps filter out the bad side effects in our life. It helps us to turn the negative into the positive. As we become wiser, we will begin to eliminate some people from our life because they bring horrible side effects. They cause more harm than good, they cause more stress than happiness, and they are the foundation of our misery because misery loves company.

They hate to see us change gears by stepping completely out of the way and allowing God to be our solid foundation. Those bad side effects could be closer to home and they are really contagious. The cure is to dare to be different, carry our cross, and along the way, learn how to trust God.

While on vacation my little one wanted me to teach him how to swim. He would hesitate to learn how to float because of his fear of the deep water. His fear reminded me of how so many people are afraid to trust God.

I humbly explained to my son that he had to trust the water, and it was his friend. Being fearful of trusting the water, he was afraid to kick his legs, let alone move his arms. As he kept taking the short cut, pretending he was swimming by walking forward and moving his hands, I saw the disappointment in his eyes. I pulled him to the side and told him,

"You look disappointed because you know you are cheating yourself." The worst thing we can do is cheat ourselves and know we are doing so.

Going down someone else's path or taking a short cut is going to take us longer than intended because those paths are not made for us. God has His own path that He made exactly for us, and it is unique. My son said, "Mom, I should trust the water, because the water is my friend." I repeated it for him over and over again until he began to float.

Just as my son had to trust the water and realize that the water was his friend, we have to trust God and believe in Him because He is more than a friend.

Jesus told him, "Don't be afraid; just believe" (Mark 5:36).

He is our Guidance, Deliverer, and Redeemer. We have to trust and know He will not let us drown; and when we are tired from kicking, He will keep us afloat. There are no side effects when it comes to trusting our trustworthy Father in heaven. With that being said, we cannot be afraid to dismiss our bad side effects; they are the ones that keep us from conquering our journey.

They are the reason why you take a U-turn, or go down the wrong path. The number one cure is to let God take charge. You will be amazed how things will start to fall into place once you take up your cross and follow Him.

After we follow up with God, the ending results will be an earned crown and hearing God say, "Well done, my child, well done!" When our cross is too heavy to bear, we need to always remember to maintain our trust in God and know He can do anything but fail.

Most Faithful One,

Thank You for every cross I have to bear, for I would not be who I am today if I did not take up each cross. As I carried each cross, in the time of weakness You were my strength. When I carried each cross in the time of sorrow and pain, You healed me. Thank You for always stepping in right on time. Amen.

❧14❧

EMBRACING CHANGE

Always giving thanks to God the Father for everything, in the name of our Lord Jesus Christ (Ephesians 5:20).

God's divine grace and mercy are sufficient. His words are so powerful; they are exactly what we need to feed our hunger and to quench our thirst. The Word of God should be soaked into our brain like a sponge soaks in liquid. Instead of overwhelming ourselves with worries and being consumed with stress, we should overwhelm ourselves with God's divine benefit, which is His word to gain wisdom. We will be able to let go of the grip of worrying about tomorrow.

Therefore do not worry about tomorrow, for tomorrow will worry about itself. Each day has enough trouble of its own (Matthew 6:34).

If we overwhelm ourselves with the Word, miraculously it changes our way of thinking and our anxiety will not paralyze us. Our fear will not hold us back from being victorious warriors. Change will be visible around us, and we will notice sooner rather than later that His divine love will unfold and multiply more than we could imagine. We will find ourselves worrying less, and our fears will gradually disappear. The grip we once had on our worries will shift gears, and we will be able to focus on the Word.

When I had many sleepless nights, I prayed for myself and for everyone who was going through a rougher situation than me. I found myself struggling, holding on to nothing, and heading in all kinds of directions.

Do not be anxious about anything, but in every situation, by prayer and petition, with thanksgiving, present in your requests to God; and the peace of God, which transcends all understanding, will guard your hearts and your minds in Christ; Finally, brothers and sisters, whatever is true, whatever is noble, whatever is right, whatever is pure, whatever is lovely, whatever is admirable—if anything is excellent or praiseworthy—think about such things (Philippians 4:6-8).

There were times when I thought I was going to lose my mind because my trouble and worries were getting the best of me. Not only that, I was filled with resentment, and not knowing how to forgive took control over my life. My life was a combination of a tsunami, tornado, earthquake, and a hurricane.

I did not understand why my life was in full of darkness or why I was suffering and everyone around me, including my ex-husband, was prospering. I asked God time and time again why my ex-husband was enjoying life when he was the one who ran out on our family.

I asked God, "Why is it, after all the hurt and pain, You allow him to face me when I was at my lowest?" I felt betrayed because my ex-husband had on the finest clothes, was driving the latest car, and he was happy and in the process of planning a wedding. I asked God how He could bless him, when I was the one left in the storm trying to figure out how my children and I were going to survive.

I questioned God how He could allow him to get married

again when the doors wasn't properly closed from his previous marriage. I asked God why He was making a complete fool of me.

I felt helpless because I thought God was making fun and mocking me. I asked God why I was being punished and why did He turn His back on me. I did not feel loved by God and honestly, I thought He forgot about my children and me because my ex-husband was living the life of freedom and luxury, while I was struggling.

Therefore we do not lose heart. Though outwardly we are wasting away; yet inwardly we are being renewed day by day. For our light and momentary troubles are achieving for us an external glory that for outweighs them all. So we fix our eyes not what is seen, but on what is unseen, since what is seen is temporary, but what is unseen is external (2 Corinthians 4:16-18).

What made matters worse was that I was listening to some of my family members and friends who did not make it any better with their advice. Most of them were happy to see that my marriage failed and see me struggle, starting from ground zero.

I had to surround myself with positive people, which weren't even a handful. I kept most of my problems to myself and I realized there was only one person to turn to—that person was God.

When I stopped listening to other people and directed my attention solely to God and His word, my damaged wounds began healing slowly but surely. Although the dark clouds were still visible, I saw the sun peeking out to shine a couple rays that gave me a little light.

God is not human, that He should lie, not a human being, that
He should change His mind. Does He speak and them not act?
Does He promise and not fulfill? (Numbers 23:19).

The weight of my struggles was too heavy to bear. I had
to let go and let God be the foundation of my life. When I
focused on the Word, started writing in my journal, and
stopped focusing on my problems, my wounds healed so that
the scabs were not even visible.

I prepared myself to face the challenges life dealt me and
face them head on without fear, doubt, shame, or emotional
burden. Each day was a fight, but I gained strength from each
battle. My mind became sharpened with each rejection, my
soul became renewed with each falling tear, and my actions
were more visible than my words.

I was not afraid of change because I refused to be content
and comfortable. Every day when I awakened, I yearned for
change. I molded my mind to embrace change, to accept each
struggle as it made me wiser, stronger, a doer, and to stand
when anything evil dared to come by way.

Do not be afraid. Stand firm and you will see the deliverance of
the Lord will bring you today (Exodus 14:13).

Being torn in a magnitude of directions was not an option because God was now my compass. When I look back at
my situation, I knew God did not walk out or turn His back
on me. He was preparing me to suit up for the greatest moments of my life. I learned constructive action serves a purpose. He had a plan for me and I couldn't succeed with the
plan if I did not execute my trials.

Faith is very powerful. During my tribulation, I gathered
along the way what I wanted to achieve. In order to accom-
plish achievement, I learned I must first mentally conceive a

plan, proceed with actions, and know and have confidence that God was my blueprint.

But when you ask, you must believe and not doubt, because the one who doubts is like a wave of the sea, blown and tossed by the wind (James 1:6).

He guided me on daily basics of how to think, what to say, and which path to take.

I desired peace daily, and peace was with me day and night. When people crossed my path, they would tell me to keep smiling because I made their day. Little did they know the battles I was facing, but I was and am a fighter. Their compliments made my day as well.

God was using strangers to rejuvenate me by their refreshing words. I found myself sleeping with a confidence that healed and repaired my mind, body, and soul. As I started each day, each step I took was a step of confidence and pride. God was creating a new and improved Charlena.

Yet this I call to mind and therefore I have hope; because of the Lord's great love we are not consumed, for His compassion never fail; They are new every morning great is your faithfulness (Lamentations 3:21-23).

When my family and friends looked at me, they couldn't recognize me. They were used to seeing the old Charlena who was standing on the edge. They looked surprised to see a newly revived and fully developed Charlena.

I learned from my mistakes, and I raised my standards to pray according to God's will, never letting anyone have the authority to shatter my confidence or self-esteem.

Do not conform to the pattern of this world, but be transformed by the renewing of your mind. Then you will be able to test and approve what God's will is—His good, pleasing and perfect will (Romans 12:2).

From positive patterns embrace change and never be afraid of battles for they make us better, wiser, and stronger people by God's grace and mercy.

God's unconditional love turned me into a believer that there is always a solution to any problem, and that the solution is already on the way. His love enabled me to overcome my problems by my becoming aware of my surroundings and the unwelcome visitors I invited in my life.

I learned I should not take commitments lightly or put other interests above my own when I knew it would only hurt me in the long run. When I started to put God first, reading my journals helped me realize how far I came, and my purpose in life my life changed tremendously for the better.

When I once again realized I mattered, I was smiling, full of laughter, peace, and serenity. I enjoyed life and my worries faded in the background. I had my share of challenges, but they did not get the best of me. I prayed about them and placed them at God's feet. I learned that I cannot worry about the things I cannot change.

Now faith is confidence in what we hope for and assurance about what we do not see (Hebrews 11:1).

I had faith and my heart was full of hope because I knew God already had it worked out. I didn't have time to fear because I knew, without a doubt, God was directing my path. If the road wasn't His will, I knew His will would be done.

I couldn't worry about what I thought was failure. I knew that my failures would be lessons learned that would produce growth. Nowadays, when things are out of my control such as my financial situation, family issues, or life in general, I will say, "Lord I am leaving this situation in Your hands, for I do not know what to do, but I do know I am not going to worry because You have it under control."

So that your faith might not rest on human wisdom, but on God's power (1 Corinthians 2:5).

I have been through so much, and worrying only gave me headaches, heart pains, stress, wear and tear on my body, and sleepless nights. It kept me in the darkness; I was unhappy, frustrated, confused, and unsettled. After all these years, I have finally learned God is the maintenance man because He is the One who can fix and clean house. In order to let God lead the way, it is important that our spiritual lives are rooted, stable, and grounded in Him.

Sometimes in order for God to be the foundation of our lives, we can't always be the star player. We have to sit on the sidelines to replenish what we've lost. He will restore and recharge our mind and soul by calming the storm in our life.

The greatest comfort in sorrow we could ever ask for is God's divine great peace. When the storm is out of control and unbearable, God's unconditional love will help us to be able to gain a level of incredible knowledge without losing the joy in life. We will be able to make sober decisions, which will be the most memorable and greatest moments in our lives.

Sometimes we are broken to be made new because we have a new purpose that God want us to conquer. When things seem to be impossible, we need to always remember the presence of God is within and around us at all times. When the impossible doesn't seem to be possible, we need to brace ourselves to not fret or fear, but instead pay close attention to the difficult hills that are placed before us.

We must trust and accept God's gift to us. The journey is not always an easy and light road to travel. God will give us strength and will take us places we have never been and show us things we never have seen before. He will give us the courage and strength to become strong conquerors. As our challenges become tough, we have to keep an open mind and keep pressing forward to achieve our purpose.

When our life becomes troublesome and unpredictable, and some things are unclear, we wonder what our next move should be. That is when we must be still and wait in hope.

The Lord will fight for you; you need only you be still (Exodus 14:14).

As we read in Exodus 14:10-22, God will plan an unexpected route for His people. Sometimes it can become frustrating because it seems these challenges are never ending. Sooner or later they will come to an end. Our challenges are not the enemy. They help us take charge; once we take charge, it creates discipline. As we are disciplined, we have a choice to let our breakthrough confine us or to embrace change.

Nothing stays the same; our life has different seasons. As the season's change, we should embrace change, stay grounded, and be willing to make decisions that move things forward and not backwards. We all can make room for change. Embracing change is a form of growth, and we should not be afraid to be redirected to do or be someone better. Once we accept and embrace change, we will see immediate results to build a better future and have peace in and around us.

Embracing change helps us appreciate the little things

that we think of less often, which are our self-worth; we cannot have peace if we do not value our worth. A peace of mind will be complemented by positive patterns such as love, happiness, joy, and a superior personality. A superior personality will give us the ability to be cautious by giving us the knowledge and understanding to look before we leap.

As we let God guide us without limitation, there will be new horizons, regardless if the water seems too deep or the mountains seem too steep.

> *"For the mountains may depart and the hills be removed, but My steadfast love shall not depart from you, and my covenant of peace shall not be removed," says the Lord, who has compassion on you* (Isaiah 54:10).

We will not hesitate to take the leap because we know our Father is with us when we break free of unwelcomed visitors, as our seasons change. The source of hope of forgiveness will set us free as we embrace change.

Forgiveness allows us to develop self-discipline and helps us to let go of toxic attachments to people, places, materials things, or even ourselves. It helps us to inherit and visualize how to focus on the effort.

The rewards are knowing there is no need to grow weary because our enemies do not have the upper hand; there is no need to become discouraged because God has everything worked out in advance. Most importantly, God is our peace and joy, and nothing can make us believe otherwise.

When we leave the past behind, we should learn from it and forgive those who despitefully used and abused us. We then can calm our souls because the best is yet to come. We can finally focus on God's unfailing love and all of His bountiful benefits.

Praise the Lord, my soul; all my inmost being, praise His holy name. Praise the Lord, my soul, and forget not all His benefits—who forgives all your sins and heals all your disease; Who redeems your life from the pit and crowns you with love and compassion; Who satisfies your desires with good things so that your youth is renewed like the eagle's (Psalm 103:1-5).

We should give our worries to God and start thanking Him for what we have, instead of focusing on what we do not have. We should thank Him for our situation because He is setting us up for something spectacular.

When we feel like giving up and when all else has failed and collapsed, we have to keep the faith and know that with God all things are possible.

In our darkest hours He will always make a way. It is time to take up our cross, charge into the battle, and fight a good fight. We cannot lose because we have God on our side and are rid of our unwelcome visitors that do more harm than good.

Brothers and sisters, I do not consider myself yet to have taken hold of it. But one thing I do: Forgetting what is behind and straining towards what is ahead; I press on towards the goal to win the prize for which God has called me heavenward in Christ (Philippians 3:13-14).

Press forward and keep your mind focused on God. Through your trials and tribulations, He will give you peace, He will be your Comforter, and He will be your Deliverance.

Most Powerful,

I cannot thank You enough for all of what You have done for me. Your love is like no other from the mountain top to the core in the bottom of the deep sea. How amazing to know Your love has no limitation or boundaries! It is an honor to be loved by You, for no one can love me unconditionally as You do. Thank You for being my Rock, my Provider, my Protector, and my Peace. Amen.

About the Author

Charlena Jackson's positive attitude has encouraged many people to pray, keep the faith, and always turn the negative into the positive. Charlena earned her Bachelors in Biology, her first Masters in Sport Health Science, her second Masters in Healthcare Administration, and she is currently working on her PhD in Healthcare Administration. Charlena is a much loved inspirational speaker. Charlena and her three children reside in Atlanta, Georgia, where Charlena is a professor at a university in Georgia.